T0091644

3D Printed Science Projects Volume 2

Physics, Math, Engineering and Geology Models

Joan Horvath
Rich Cameron

Apress®

3D Printed Science Projects Volume 2: Physics, Math, Engineering and Geology Models

Joan Horvath
Nonscriptum LLC, Pasadena, California, USA

Rich Cameron
Nonscriptum LLC, Pasadena, California, USA

ISBN-13 (pbk): 978-1-4842-2694-0
DOI 10.1007/978-1-4842-2695-7

ISBN-13 (electronic): 978-1-4842-2695-7

Copyright © 2017 by Joan Horvath and Rich Cameron

This work is subject to copyright. All rights are reserved by the Publisher, whether the whole or part of the material is concerned, specifically the rights of translation, reprinting, reuse of illustrations, recitation, broadcasting, reproduction on microfilms or in any other physical way, and transmission or information storage and retrieval, electronic adaptation, computer software, or by similar or dissimilar methodology now known or hereafter developed. Exempted from this legal reservation are brief excerpts in connection with reviews or scholarly analysis or material supplied specifically for the purpose of being entered and executed on a computer system, for exclusive use by the purchaser of the work. Duplication of this publication or parts thereof is permitted only under the provisions of the Copyright Law of the Publisher's location, in its current version, and permission for use must always be obtained from Springer. Permissions for use may be obtained through RightsLink at the Copyright Clearance Center. Violations are liable to prosecution under the respective Copyright Law.

Trademarked names, logos, and images may appear in this book. Rather than use a trademark symbol with every occurrence of a trademarked name, logo, or image we use the names, logos, and images only in an editorial fashion and to the benefit of the trademark owner, with no intention of infringement of the trademark.

The use in this publication of trade names, trademarks, service marks, and similar terms, even if they are not identified as such, is not to be taken as an expression of opinion as to whether or not they are subject to proprietary rights.

The models described in this book (but not the book itself) are licensed under a Creative Commons Attribution -ShareAlike 4.0 International license.

While the advice and information in this book are believed to be true and accurate at the date of publication, neither the authors nor the editors nor the publisher can accept any legal responsibility for any errors or omissions that may be made. The publisher makes no warranty, express or implied, with respect to the material contained herein.

Managing Director: Welmoed Spahr
Editorial Director: Todd Green
Lead Editor: Natalie Pao
Coordinating Editor: Jessica Vakili
Copy Editor: Corbin Collins

Distributed to the book trade worldwide by Springer Science+Business Media New York, 233 Spring Street, 6th Floor, New York, NY 10013. Phone 1-800-SPRINGER, fax (201) 348-4505, e-mail orders-ny@springer-sbm.com, or visit www.springeronline.com. Apress Media, LLC is a California LLC and the sole member (owner) is Springer Science + Business Media Finance Inc (SSBM Finance Inc). SSBM Finance Inc is a **Delaware** corporation.

For information on translations, please e-mail rights@apress.com, or visit www.apress.com.

Apress and friends of ED books may be purchased in bulk for academic, corporate, or promotional use. eBook versions and licenses are also available for most titles. For more information, reference our Special Bulk Sales–eBook Licensing web page at www.apress.com/bulk-sales.

Any source code or other supplementary material referenced by the author in this book is available to readers on GitHub via the book's product page, located at www.apress.com/978-1-4842-2694-0. For more detailed information, please visit http://www.apress.com/source-code.

Printed on acid-free paper

To Steve Unwin, for encouragement, patience, and physics

Contents at a Glance

Contents

About the Authors

Joan Horvath and **Rich Cameron** are the cofounders of Nonscriptum LLC, based in Pasadena, California. Nonscriptum consults for educational and scientific users in the areas of 3D printing and maker technologies. Joan and Rich find ways to use maker tech to teach science and math in a hands-on way, and want to make scientific research cheaper and more accessible to the public.

This book is their sixth collaboration for Apress, and it particularly builds on their earlier *3D Printed Science Projects* (Apress, 2016). They also teach online classes in 3D printing and maker tech for LERN Network's U Got Class continuing education program. Links for all of the above are on their website, www.nonscriptum.com.

In addition to her work with Rich, Joan also has an appointment as core adjunct faculty for National University's College of Letters and Sciences. She has taught at the university level in a variety of institutions, both in Southern California and online. Before she and Rich started Nonscriptum, she held a variety of entrepreneurial positions, including VP of business development at a Kickstarter-funded 3D-printer company. Joan started her career with 16 years at the NASA/Caltech Jet Propulsion Laboratory, where she worked in programs including the technology transfer office, the Magellan spacecraft to Venus, and the TOPEX/Poseidon oceanography spacecraft. She holds an undergraduate degree from MIT in aeronautics and astronautics and a master's degree in engineering from UCLA.

Rich (known online as "Whosawhatsis") is an experienced open source developer who has been a key member of the RepRap 3D-printer development community for many years. His designs include the original spring/lever extruder mechanism used on many 3D printers, the RepRap Wallace, and the Deezmaker Bukito portable 3D printer. By building and modifying several of the early open source 3D printers to wrestle unprecedented performance out of them, he has become an expert at maximizing the print quality of filament-based printers. When he's not busy making every aspect of his own 3D printers better, from slicing software to firmware and hardware, he likes to share that knowledge and experience online so that he can help make everyone else's printers better too.

Acknowledgments

The consumer 3D-printing ecosystem would not exist in its current form without the open source 3D printing hardware and software community. This is particularly true of Marius Kintel, the main developer and maintainer of OpenSCAD software, and his collaborators, for their software which was used to develop the objects in this book. We are also grateful for the support of the MatterHackers team and their MatterControl software, particular Lars Brubaker, Kevin Pope, and Mara Hitner. The maker community as a whole has also been very supportive. The picture of Joan and Rich in the "About the Authors" section was taken at the 2015 San Mateo Makerfaire by Ethan Etnyre; we appreciate how much we have been inspired by looking at projects made by everyone at maker events large and small.

The Apress production team was there for us to solve problems as they arose and let us have great creative freedom otherwise. We dealt most directly with Natalie Pao, Jessica Vakili, Corbin Collins, and Welmoed Spahr, but we also appreciate the many we did not see.

We picked a lot of scientists' brains as we thought about how to model some of the concepts in this book. Joan's astronomer husband, Stephen Unwin (to whom this book is dedicated as a long-overdue thanks), was a huge help as we reminded ourselves about all the basic physics we had forgotten. Frank Carsey, Sue Digby, members of the LIGO team (particularly Alan Weinstein at Caltech), and many others helped us out by reading a chapter draft or giving us some of their time to discuss their science.

We were inspired to create 3D-printable educational models originally by discussions with people in the community of teachers of the visually impaired, notably Mike Cheverie, Lore Schindler, and Yue-Ting Siu.

Finally, we are grateful to our families for putting up with our endless brainstorming, kitchen table commandeering, and test runs of explanations. As always, we learned a lot writing this book, and we hope you will get as much out of reading it and playing with the models as we did creating it.

Introduction

When we wrote our first book of 3D-printable science projects, we knew that students, parents, and teachers would get excited about using a 3D printer, might download a 3D model, print it, and then wonder what to do next. Or they might get into creating models from scratch and become discouraged by the limitations of easier 3D modeling programs or the learning curves of the more capable ones.

In our first book, we created a middle path: models that you could just print but that would be reasonably easy to alter if you wanted to do more. Further, we designed the models so that they would be useful to learn science or math principles by changing their features. In particular, we wanted to create some seeds of science fair or extra-credit projects—that is, open-ended, meaty explorations that could be explored at a variety of levels. In that first book, we were surprised at how hard this turned out to be. Most textbooks and online sites endlessly recycle versions of the same 2D projection of models of science concepts.

You would think we would have learned better by now and that we would be able to just sit back, crack our knuckles, and pound out a model in an afternoon or so. Not even close. As with the first book, in each chapter we have a "Learning Like a Maker" section where we talk about our adventures in defining and implementing the models.

Some of the deceptively simple models (like the pendulums in Chapter 1 and weighted wheel in Chapter 5) actually involve some subtle physics to make them work well at a tabletop scale. For the interactive models that can be used for some simple demonstrations, we tried to use measuring equipment that pretty much anyone would have in their home, supplemented by free smartphone apps. This sometimes made accurate-enough measurement challenging, and we talk about how to deal with that in each case.

Speaking of accurate measurement, we were excited to create a simplified model of one of the biggest scientific observations in recent memory: gravitational waves (Chapter 8). We enjoyed the challenge of wringing out approximations that would preserve some behavior while not taking users into complicated exercises in downloading output of scientific user models (although we encourage you to use our model as inspiration and move on to endeavors along those lines!)

This book presumes you know a little bit about 3D printing already. If you don't, Appendix A and the resources linked there should get you up to speed. The models are all written using the OpenSCAD free and open source 3D modeling program. If you know how to program in a language like C, Java, or Python, that will help but is not strictly necessary to alter the models. Appendix A and the OpenSCAD materials linked there will help you out with that too.

We have found that teachers use 3D printers in one of two fundamental ways: either they want to create a model to pass around in class to help students visualize a concept, or they want students to use a printer either to learn engineering and design per se or to do classroom explorations of physical concepts such as moment of inertia. Since most of these models lend themselves to being used in many different ways, we have not included a grade level or explicit lesson plans.

To show our readers who are teachers (in the United States) what we had in mind, though, at the end of most chapters we suggest Next Generation Science Standards that we thought might benefit from these models. These science standards, from the group NGSS Lead States, are documented in *Next Generation Science Standards: For States, By States* (The National Academies Press, 2013). Links are given at the end of relevant chapters.

We do not pretend to be experts in K-12 education, but we looked through the standards as engineers to find the best fit in our opinion from the technical practitioner point of view. If you are a teacher, you may want to check with your state or school standards as well to see the best fit.

The models span a variety of topics, and we tried to cover as many disciplines as possible. We have aimed these at students who know some basic algebra (enough to read an equation with an exponent in it). If you know some calculus, you will understand some of the models more quickly, but you might teach yourself more if you do not! Briefly, here is what you can look forward to:

Chapter 1 discusses pendulums and allows you to create simple and compound ones.

Chapter 2 lets you create models of geological formations that can be hard to describe: synclines, anticlines, and a particular type of dune called a barchan dune.

Chapter 3 moves you to cooler climates and allows you to create an iceberg (and explore how it floats) and snowflakes.

Chapter 4 lets you explore the world of high-speed motion, with models of Doppler shift and shock waves.

Chapter 5 creates a deceptively simple wheel that you can weight with pennies to understand moment of inertia.

Chapter 6 is an exploration of topics in probability, from rolling dice in role-playing games to how to visualize the probability of two things varying at the same time.

Chapter 7 explores logic gates as puzzles to put together.

Chapter 8 allows you to print the gravitational waves coming from two black holes merging and throwing off inconceivable amounts of energy.

Finally, as we noted earlier, Appendix A reviews how to 3D print, and Appendix B aggregates all the links in the book.

You may also want to check out the models in our earlier *3D Printed Science Projects* book. Many of the models here build on those earlier ones. We note it where that is the case.

Finally, we are making the 3D-printable models used in this book (although not the book itself!) open source, licensed under a Creative Commons Attribution- ShareAlike 4.0 International License (https://creativecommons.org/licenses/by-sa/4.0/). That means you can use them for any purpose and alter and remix them as long as you credit us, and any derivativatives you distribute must carry the same license. In Appendix A we have some notes about where to find the repositories if you would like to add to these models. We hope these models are just the first iteration of a set of learning tools that students everywhere can play with and learn from for a long time to come.

CHAPTER 1

■ ■ ■

Pendulums

This chapter looks at the deceptively simple world of pendulums. First we cover why pendulums swing back and forth as they do, and tie this into the general idea of simple harmonic motion—a type of oscillatory motion in which a system stores energy (in a spring or by working against gravity) and then uses that stored energy to move back to its original position.

Some of the experiments in this chapter are classic high school or undergraduate physics demonstrations, and in some cases would benefit from non-3D-printed parts. However, if you do not have access to typical school lab items, you can still do some respectable explorations with the parts we give you in this chapter, plus a pair of chairs and some string. We point out possible upgrades as we go.

This chapter (like all the others in this book) first lays out a bit of science background and then develops 3D-printable models that explore these concepts. We talk about what we learned just by the process of creating the model, and finally give some tips about how you might use these models to teach the topics they demonstrate. The models are available for download from the link on the copyright page of this book.

Simple Harmonic Motion

What makes a pendulum swing back and forth, or a ball on a spring boing back and forth? *Simple harmonic motion* is a phenomenon that occurs when something moves in a way that converts energy from *potential energy* to *kinetic energy* and back again. In an ideal world, the sum of something's kinetic energy plus its potential energy is always a constant. If you raise something up high, it has potential energy. It is not moving, but you had to expend energy to get it where it is. When you let go, it falls—converting this potential energy into kinetic energy, the energy of motion. When it hits the ground, it dissipates that energy into making a big hole or cloud of dust.

But simple harmonic motion is about conversion of potential into kinetic energy in a ***back and forth*** way. Suppose you have a table built into the wall. Imagine that you have a big spring attached to the wall, with a heavy ball attached in turn to the spring and resting on the table. If you stretch the spring by pulling the ball away from the wall, and then let go, it will bounce back and forth for a while across the table. It is oscillating because you stretched the spring to start things off (storing potential energy in the spring).

© Joan Horvath and Rich Cameron 2017
J. Horvath and R. Cameron, *3D Printed Science Projects Volume 2*,
DOI 10.1007/978-1-4842-2695-7_1

When you let go, the spring converted that potential energy into kinetic energy (motion). It will likely then compress the spring and stop when the spring is compressed by the same amount that you stretched it initially, and then shoot back out. This process will continue until friction and air resistance bring it to a stop.

■ **Note**   The principle that the force needed to compress or extend a spring is proportional to the distance the spring is extended or compressed is called *Hooke's Law*. British physicist Robert Hooke proposed it over three and a half centuries ago, in 1660.

It is pretty easy to think about a mass on a spring oscillating back and forth on a table as an example of trading off potential and kinetic energy. But what about a pendulum swinging back and forth without any external forces on it (other than being pulled to one side to start the motion)? The more you pull the pendulum bob to one side, the more potential energy you are giving it because you are also raising it. When you let go, the mass will fall (converting some of its potential energy into kinetic energy), constrained by its string. It will have enough kinetic energy to carry the mass up to the other side, and stop, having converted all the kinetic energy back into potential energy. Air resistance and friction at the pivot point will eat away at the total energy over time, but if these can be minimized a pendulum can oscillate for a long time.

■ **Note**   The basic work on pendulums has its heritage in the work of Galileo Galilei (1564–1642), Christiaan Huygens (1629–1695), and Isaac Newton (1643–1726). Early practical applications focused on pendulum clocks. Huygens is credited with developing the first working pendulum clock.

As it turns out, the period of a simple pendulum (a weight swinging on a light string or wire) is given by the equation

$$Period = 2 * \pi * sqrt(l / g)$$

where l is the length of the string and g is the acceleration due to gravity (9.8 meters per second squared on earth). This formula only applies for swings under about 15 degrees either side of the centerline. It is an approximation that starts to become inaccurate for bigger swings. There are other terms proportional to the square (and higher powers) of the sine of this angle to the vertical. These terms are small when the sine of this angle is small, but become significant as the angle gets larger.

■ **Note**   We use the programming convention of using * to mean *multiply*, and sqrt(...) for *square root of*, plus the standard abbreviations for meters (m), centimeters (cm), and other metric quantities. Thus meters per second squared becomes m/s^2.

The important property, though, is that the period depends only on the length of the string supporting the mass and not on the mass (unlike the spring example) or any other property of the pendulum. This is why pendulums were of interest first in clocks, and later on in other investigations that we talk about a little later in this chapter.

Friction (including air resistance) will eventually stop these oscillatory motions in the real world. The existence of friction acts as a ***damping*** force which takes energy out of the system, eventually bringing it to rest. As you will read in the "Learning Like a Maker" section in this chapter, we spent a lot of time battling friction in our designs.

The Models

In this chapter we start out with a simple pendulum (a mass on a string) and then move on to ***physical*** (sometimes called ***compound***) pendulums, which are stiff parts that swings back and forth as a whole. Finally, we combine some of these to show the counterintuitive behavior of two or more simple pendulums connected together, or of a ***double pendulum***, which connects two physical pendulums. The double pendulum displays ***chaotic behavior***—seemingly-random oscilations.

■ **Tip** If you are new to 3D printing, you might want to look at Appendix A first, which talks about both 3D printing in general and using OpenSCAD in particular. All the models in this book are written in OpenSCAD. Electronic copies of all the models in this can be downloaded from the publisher's page for this book. Go to `www.apress.com` and search on this book's title to get to the correct page.

Simple Pendulum

The first model is a simple pendulum bob designed to be hung from a string. It has room for a few coins to be packed inside to weigh it down a little. It is set up to take up to four United States pennies, but there is a parameter, `coins_diameter`, which is the diameter of the desired coin, in mm. For U.S. pennies, it should be 19.5 mm; for quarters, 25 mm. If you live in other countries, you can find out the relevant coin dimension by doing an online search for the word "diameter" followed by the name of your coin. Add about half a millimeter to the actual diameter to allow for imprecision and some tolerance to allow the coins to be inserted and removed easily. The simple pendulum model (sized for pennies) is shown in Figure 1-1.

Figure 1-1. *The simple pendulum*

■ **Caution**   Many of the models in this chapter and elsewhere in this book have small parts and should not be used around young children. Treat them as science experiments, not as toys.

To test it out, put four pennies into the hollow area. Tie a piece of string to the top of the pendulum bob, and either tie the other end to someplace where it can swing freely (for example, a curtain rod with the curtains pulled back, or held in place with a heavy book at the edge of a table, as in Figure 1-2). Next, you will need to know the distance from the center of mass of the pendulum, which we will assume is roughly at the center of the pennies. Measure from the center of the coins to where the string is free to move at the top.

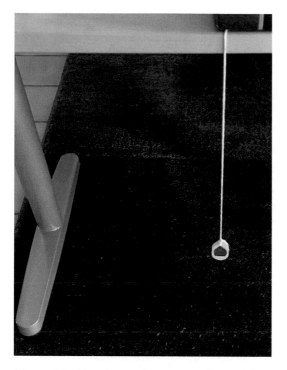

Figure 1-2. *Experimental setup, simple pendulum with a short string*

Next, pull the pendulum to one side, say 15 degrees or so from the vertical. Start a stopwatch (you probably have one in your phone's clock application) and see how long it takes for the pendulum to return 50 times to one extreme position, for example all the way to the right, and then divide by the number of oscillations. (We have the little triangle on the bottom to make it easier to see positioning.) That time it takes for the pendulum to make a full swing and back again is the ***period***. Note that the longer the string, the easier it is to measure the (slower) period.

It is a little tricky to do this measurement. Start the pendulum swinging first. Then start the stopwatch when the pendulum reaches an apex of its swing; then count the number of times it returns to that apex. We discovered that it is best to measure the actual distance of the pivot point of the string to the center of mass when the pendulum is actually hanging up—strings stretch a bit, and tying it introduces a lot of errors.

The period should be ***2 * π * sqrt(l / g)***. If we have a one-meter-long string, the period is: ***2 * 3.14159 * sqrt(1 m / 9.8 m/s²)***, or 2.0 seconds. We did two trials and got 59.9 and 59.6 seconds for 30 swings, for a period of 1.99 seconds—accurate within our ability to stop the stopwatch, measure the distance, and other parameters.

Listing 1-1 is the OpenSCAD model for this pendulum bob. If you wanted to use different coins, you would change the `coins_diameter` and `coins_depth` parameters. These should both be a little bit (a few mm) bigger than the dimensions of the stack of coins you want to have inside the bob. Note that `coins_depth` is the thickness of the coin multiplied by how many of them you want to have in there.

Listing 1-1. Simple Pendulum Model

```
// File simple_pendulum.scad
// A pendulum bob designed to carry coins
// Pendulum is pointed on the bottom for ease of reading
// Rich "Whosawhatsis" Cameron, December 2016

thick=2; // wall thickness (mm)
// should include tolerance to make coins fit easily (mm)
coins_diameter=19.5;
// use 19.5 for a US penny; 25 for a US quarter
coins_depth=8; // total depth of coins (mm); here, 4 pennies

holder=4; // controls how much the coins are covered by lip on top

$fs=.2;
$fa=2;

// First section creates the back of the model
// the flat part printed on the platform
linear_extrude(1) difference() {
    offset(thick / 2) {
        hull() for(i=[0, holder]) translate([0, -i, 0])
            circle(coins_diameter / 2);
        rotate(45) square(coins_diameter / 2); // create point on bottom
    }
    translate([0, coins_diameter / sqrt(2), 0])
        circle(coins_diameter / 2);
} //end back

// Next section creates the lip on top that keeps coins in
translate([0, 0, coins_depth+1]) linear_extrude(1) offset(thick / 2)
difference() {
    offset(thick / 2) hull() for(i=[0, holder]) translate([0, -i, 0])
        circle(coins_diameter / 2);
    translate([-coins_diameter/2 - thick / 2, -coins_diameter/2, 0])
        square(coins_diameter+thick);
} // end creation of top

// Next section creates outer wall
linear_extrude(coins_depth+2) difference() {
    offset(thick) {
        hull() for(i=[0, holder]) translate([0, -i, 0])
            circle(coins_diameter / 2);
        rotate(45) square(coins_diameter / 2);
    } // end offset
```

```
    offset(0) {
       hull() for(i=[0, holder]) translate([0, -i, 0])
          circle(coins_diameter / 2);
       rotate(45) square(coins_diameter / 2);
    } // end offset
} // end outer wall creation

// Next section creates the point at the bottom
translate([
    0,
    -coins_diameter / 2 - holder - thick,
    coins_depth / 2+1
]) rotate([90, 0, 90]) linear_extrude(thick, center=true) {
    difference() {
       union() {
          rotate(45)
             square((coins_depth+2) / sqrt(2), center=true);
          translate([0, - coins_depth / 2 - 1, 0]) square(coins_depth+2);
       } // end union
       translate([thick / 2, - coins_depth / 2 - 1, 0]) square(coins_depth+2);
    } // end difference
} // end fin at the bottom
```

Printing Tips

This model is very easy to print. If you want to make a more complex system with several pendulums, you can always print as many as you can fit on your platform at the same time. You should generally **not** use support with this model. Unless you make one a lot bigger than the penny sized one in Listing 1-1, the print should **bridge** (print over an open space between two areas) just fine. On the other hand, if you do turn on support, it will be very difficult to get the support out of there.

Coupled Pendulums

You can play with different lengths of the simple pendulum. What gets interesting is when you try out coupling a few of them—hanging several pendulums in such a way that they affect each other's motion. If you hang a string (keeping it fairly taut) between two chairs and then tie two or more pendulums to that string, you will get coupled pendulums.

First try having the two pendulums being as identical as possible (same number of pennies, same length of string). Start one moving and watch the second one take over the motion (Figure 1-3). This is the phenomenon of **resonance**—oscillating objects increasing the amplitude of their motion when they are pushed at a particular frequency.

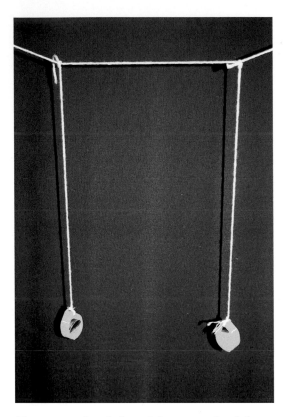

Figure 1-3. *Coupled pendulum setup. Pendulums are free to swing toward and away from the camera during the experiment. Cloth was placed behind them to make them more visible for photograph.*

As we have seen, pendulums have a natural frequency at which they will oscillate. If two pendulums are able to trade energy back and forth, as they can in the setup in Figure 1-3, each pendulum will alternate between being at rest and swinging at its natural frequency. The first pendulum gets its start when you pull it back and let go. This first pendulum, though, is going to pull on the string that supports both pendulums, and that will start to tug on the second pendulum. After a while, this will drive the second pendulum to its resonant frequency. (Note that you would pull one pendulum toward you in the setup in Figure 1-3, not side to side.)

However, the energy for this has to come from somewhere, and the other pendulum will start to oscillate at a lower and lower amplitude and may even briefly stop before it begins to speed up again. There are many videos out there of these phenomena. One we liked is at `www.youtube.com/watch?v=izy4a5erom8` from the group Sixty Symbols.

If you just have two strings of the same length and start one swinging, the two pendulums will trade motion back and forth. If, however, you go to three pendulums and/or start making them different in length, you will get variable behaviors. The math of this becomes quite complex very quickly.

Compound (Physical) Pendulum

The equation for the compound pendulum's period is similar to that of the simple pendulum, but requires two new factors: ***the moment of inertia***, commonly denoted by a capital ***I***, and the distance between the center of mass and the pivot point, which is usually called ***R***. The moment of inertia determines the torque needed to rotate a body about a particular axis (for rotation around one axis, like that we are talking about now). Figure 1-4 shows our model of a compound pendulum on the printer.

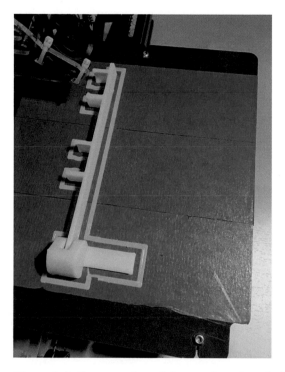

Figure 1-4. *Compound pendulum on the printer bed*

To calculate moment of inertia and the position of the center of gravity in general requires calculus (https://en.wikipedia.org/wiki/Moment_of_inertia#Compound_pendulum), but we can estimate it for a few cases. If we have a series of connected, somewhat discrete masses, it is the sum of each mass times the square of its distance from the pivot point:

$$Period = 2 * \pi * sqrt(I / (Sum\ of\ masses) * g * R)$$

So if we had two equal masses, *m* and *M*, the center of which were distances *a* and *b* from the pivot on a stiff compound pivot that is otherwise pretty light, we would get a moment of inertia of $m * a^2 + M * b^2$. Also, $m + M$ is the total mass of the pendulum, *I* is moment of inertia, and *R* is the distance from the center of mass to the pivot. When the two masses *m* and *M* are equal, the center of mass is halfway between centers of these two masses. The equation in that case becomes:

$$Period = 2 * \pi * sqrt((m * a^2 + M * b^2) / ((m + M) * g * (a + b) / 2))$$

The first entry in the array *length* in the OpenSCAD model is *a*, and *b* is the second entry. The model we are giving you here has *a* = 50 mm (0.05 m) and *b* = 100 mm (0.1 m). If *m* and *M* are each half the total mass, then the value of *R* (the center of mass relative to the pivot point) will be halfway between the two masses, or at 75 mm (0.075 m).

The actual values of the masses cancel out (only their ratios are important), and g is 9.8 m/s². Therefore, the period for this scenario is 0.58 seconds for any masses that are the same as each other.

If the mass at *M* is twice the mass at *m* (the farther mass is heavier) then the center of mass is 2/3 of the way from *a* to *b*, closer to the heavier mass. *R* becomes 50 mm (distance of the center of the first mass) plus 2/3 of the 50 mm between them, or 83.3 mm. In this case the period becomes 0.60 seconds, as befits a pendulum that is, in effect, slightly longer. If it is the other way around (the closer-in mass is twice the mass of the farther one), then *R* becomes 66.7 mm. Note that in these unequal cases the total mass in the denominator is three times the mass of the lightest one.

Testing the Compound Pendulum

We designed this model to fit even on small consumer printers. In an ideal world it would be bigger to allow for longer, easier-to-measure periods. The model has holes where you can insert pennies as weights and a flat, rectangular tab that you can place on the edge of a table. To start the pendulum, place the desired number of pennies in the holes, hold down the tab on a table or place a book on top of it, and pull the pendulum back to its stop (Figure 1-5).

Figure 1-5. *The experimental setup for the compound pendulum*

■ **Caution**   U.S. pennies changed weight in 1982, from 3 grams each to 2.5 grams. In these experiments where the mass of the pennies matters, be sure you have all one kind or the other, because results may vary otherwise.

Let go, and use the stopwatch to see how long it takes for 40 or 50 oscillations. The model slows down pretty quickly, and will probably barely be moving after about ten oscillations. Even though the motion becomes tiny, if you observe carefully you should be able to count 40 or 50 oscillations. Table 1-1 summarizes the cases we calculated earlier in detail, plus the last one for completeness.

Table 1-1. *Examples for Compound Pendulum*

Scenario	Period (seconds)
One mass centered at 0.050 mm (Use simple pendulum formula, length = 0.050 m)	0.44
One mass centered at 0.10 m (Use simple pendulum formula, length = 0.10 m)	0.63
Two equal masses, one at 0.05 m and one at 0.10 m (R = 0.075 m)	0.58
One mass at 0.05 m and one twice as heavy at 0.10 m (R = 0.083 m, and total mass = 3 times mass of lightest one)	0.60
One mass at 0.10 m and one twice as heavy at 0.050 m (R = 0.067 m and total mass = 3 times mass of lightest one)	0.55

Realistically you will probably only be able to get general trends. If you have a bigger printer, you might increase the values of the length array to have a longer pendulum. Do not just scale it, though, because the pivot at the top might not work, and the coins may fall out. Also, the pendulum is not really one or two masses connected by massless plastic. Your values may vary a bit depending on your print settings, the type of plastic, and so on.

Listing 1-2 lays out the model, which can be configured to have muliple sets of coins spread out along its length.

Listing 1-2. Compound Pendulum Model

```
// File compound_pendulum.scad
// A rigid pendulum meant to carry multiple sets of coins
// Rich "Whosawhatsis" Cameron, December 2016

width=10; // width in mm, parallel to coins
thick=2; // thickness in mm
length=[50, 100]; // in mm from the pivot.
// array of positions of the center of coin holders,
// to have more holders, add more values to the length array.
coins_diameter=19.1; // in mm
// 19.1 is US pennies plus a small tolerance
coins_depth=8; // depth of coin holder; this is for 4 US pennies

pivot_spacing=.4; // tolerance, mm around pivot

base_len=25;
// length of the base that sticks out to attach to the table

stop_angle=25; // degrees; maximum extent of swing

$fs=.2;
$fa=2;
```

```
difference() { //fulcrum for pendulum
    union() {
        // create piece that sticks out to place on table
        translate([0, -width / 2, 0])
            cube([width / 2+thick+base_len, width, thick]);
        // create body of the fulcrum piece
        rotate([0, -90, 180]) linear_extrude(
            width+thick * 2,
            center=true,
            convexity=5
        ) union() {
            translate([width / 2, 0, 0]) intersection() {
                circle(width / sqrt(2)+2+thick);
                union() {
                    translate([-width / 2, 0, 0])
                        square([width, max(length)]);
                    rotate(45) translate([0, -width / sqrt(2), 0])
                        square([width * 2, width * sqrt(2)]);
                }
            }
            translate([width / 2, 0, 0]) intersection() {
                circle(width / sqrt(2));
                square([width, width * sqrt(2)], center=true);
            }
        } // end of body
    }

    // create cutout for conical pivot
    rotate([0, -90, 0]) translate([width / 2, 0, 0]) for(i=[0, 1])
        mirror([0, 0, i]) cylinder(
            r=width / 2+1,
            r2=0,
            h=width / 2+pivot_spacing
        );
    //create cutout for pendulum swing angle
    rotate([0, -90, 0]) linear_extrude(thick+2, center=true) {
        translate([width / 2, 0, 0]) circle(width / sqrt(2)+2);
        hull() for(a=[-stop_angle, 0, stop_angle])
            translate([width / 2, 0, 0]) rotate(a+90)
                translate([-width / 2, 0, 0])
                    square([width, max(length)]);
    } // end of swing cutout
} // end fulcrum

// create conical pivots
rotate([0, -90, 0]) translate([width / 2, 0, 0]) for(i=[0, 1])
    mirror([0, 0, i]) cylinder(r=width / 2, r2=0, h=width / 2);

// create the body of the pendulum
rotate([0, -90, 0]) linear_extrude(thick, center=true) {
```

13

```
    square([width, max(length)]);
    translate([width / 2, 0, 0]) intersection() {
        circle(width / sqrt(2));
        square([width, width * sqrt(2)], center=true);
    }
    for(i=length, d=coins_diameter+thick * 2) {
        translate([width / 2, i, 0]) intersection() {
            circle(d / sqrt(2));
            square([width, d * sqrt(2)], center=true);
        }
    }
}

rotate([0, -90, 0]) { // create coin holders
    for(i=length, d=coins_diameter+thick * 2) {
        translate([width / 2, i, 0]) difference() {
            linear_extrude(thick / 2+coins_depth+2) intersection() {
                circle(d / 2);
                square([width, d], center=true);
            }
            rotate_extrude() difference() {
                translate([0, 0, 0])
                    square([d / 2 - thick, thick / 2+coins_depth+5]);
                translate([
                    d / 2 - thick+.5,
                    thick / 2+coins_depth+1,
                    0
                ]) circle(1);
            }
        }
    }
} // end coin holders
```

Printing Tips

This model has some tight tolerances in the pivot. You may need to clean out the space around the pivot a bit. Be careful not to warp the pendulum if you do that. You will need to work the pendulum back and forth for a while to get rid of any residual plastic that is hanging things up or causing friction.

Make sure you have support turned off. You can use a skirt for this, but should avoid using a brim since it might clog up the free motion of the pendulum.

Double Pendulum

Finally, we have created a model for a *double pendulum*. This is a pair of rigid pendulums, connected so that each of the two can rotate freely. These pendulums have the property that their motion is ***chaotic***—that is, very dependent on initial conditions in ways that are hard to calculate.

The motion can be pretty unpredictable. It will not move for very long because of friction, but if you can get a clean print it will do some impressive moves for a little while. (Expect the lower arm to thrash back and forth, possibly more than 360 degrees.)

There are some great examples on YouTube. For instance, the one at www.youtube. com/watch?v=AwTOkO9w-jw starts off with about a minute-long demonstration of different non-chaotic versions of the pendulums and then moves on to the interesting stuff. If you search YouTube for "double pendulum" you will find more.

This is a little tricky to pull off with 3D printing (because it is difficult to create a small low-friction joint), and our model made a lot of tradeoffs between the desire to fit on smaller 3D printers and design of a low-friction joint.

Figure 1-6 shows the pendulum on the printer bed. The small C-shaped items are snap rings. You will slide them onto the notches on the pendulum pivots from the side to keep the arms from sliding off the end. Figures 1-7 and 1-8 show the double pendulum in use. To start it, hold both arms up, as shown in Figure 1-7, and let go. We show the pendulum held down with a heavy book; you might just want to hold it down on a tabletop and be sure you are standing clear of anywhere it might go. Put the shorter one on the bottom. There is another pivot on the bottom in case you want to try it with the bigger piece on the bottom (the behavior is less interesting that way, though). The OpenSCAD model is in Listing 1-3.

▪ **Note**   There is a third snap ring in case you break one getting it off the platform. You may have to trim it a bit if your printer "strings" across the opening. It should come out shaped like a C, not an O. The clamp should be put on from the side, not over the top, and fit into the groove on the pivot. You can see this in the front view of the pivot in Figure 1-7.

Figure 1-6. *Double pendulum as printed. Stringing inside the snap rings needs to be removed.*

Figure 1-7. *Double pendulum in starting position*

Figure 1-8. *Double pendulum in motion*

Printing Tips

Make sure the first few layers of the snap rings are complete and not peeling off the platform (restart and try again if so). Watch your first few layers for "stringing" (threads across the holes). If you have excessive stringing, you may need to change your printer's retraction settings. If you are reluctant to do that, you can ream out the holes gently with a small metal tool (like a screwdriver) that fits into the holes, or gently snip clip them if you have a small enough tool for the job. Wear eye protection when cleaning up prints because small bits tend to go flying.

Listing 1-3. The Double Pendulum

```
// File double_pendulum.scad
// A 3D printable double pendulum model
// Rich "Whosawhatsis" Cameron, December 2016

lengths=[100, 70]; // mm, length of each pendulum
width=10; // mm, width of each piece
pivot=5; // mm, diameter of the pivot center
gap=.3; // mm, spacing between pivot center and hole
thick=6; // mm, thickness of each piece
base=30; // mm, length of the base that rests on the edge of a table

$fs=.2;
$fa=2;

// create the base piece
translate([len(lengths) * (width+2), - (thick+5) / 2, 0]) {
    linear_extrude(thick) square([width, base], center=true);
    // create sideways pivot with flat side for printing
    intersection() {
        translate([0, base / 2 - thick, pivot / 2 / sqrt(2)]) {
            rotate([-90, 0, 0]) rotate_extrude() {
                difference() {
                    square([pivot / 2, thick * 2+5]);
                    translate([
                        pivot / 2+1 - sqrt(2) / 2,
                        thick * 2+3,
                        0
                    ]) circle(1);
                }
            }
        }
        linear_extrude(pivot) difference() { // flat side
            square([width, base+thick * 2+10], center=true);
        }
    } // end sideways pivot
} // end base piece
```

```
// create the pendulums
for(j=[0:len(lengths) - 1], l=lengths[j]) {
    translate([j * (width+2), 0, 0]) {
        linear_extrude(thick) difference() { // create pivot body
            hull() for(i=[.5, -.5])
                translate([0, i * l, 0]) circle(width / 2);
            translate([0, -.5 * l, 0]) circle(pivot / 2+gap);
        } // end pivot body
        // create pivot
        translate([0, .5 * l, 0]) rotate_extrude() difference() {
            square([pivot / 2, thick * 2+5]);
            translate([pivot / 2+1 - sqrt(2) / 2, thick * 2+3, 0])
            circle(1);
        }
    } // end pivot
} // end pendulums

//create the snap rings to hold the pendulums in place
for(j=[0:len(lengths)]) translate([
    -width / 2 - (pivot / 2+1 - sqrt(2) / 2) - 4,
    (j - (len(lengths)) / 2) * ((pivot / 2+1 - sqrt(2) / 2) * 2+5),
    0
]) {
    difference() { // create bendable partial ring
        rotate_extrude() intersection() {
            hull() for(i=[0, 1]) translate([
                pivot / 2+1 - sqrt(2) / 2+i,
                sqrt(2) / 2,
                0])
            circle(1);
            square([pivot / 2+1 - sqrt(2) / 2+2, sqrt(2)]);
        }
        for(i=[1, -1]) rotate(-45+15 * i) translate([0, 0, -1])
            cube(max(pivot, 4));
        translate([0, 0, -1]) cylinder(r=pivot / 2+1, h=4);
    } // end partial ring
    // create contact points at 120 degree intervals
    for(a=[-180:120:179]) rotate(a) {
        translate([pivot / 2+1 - sqrt(2) / 2+.5, 0, 0]) {
            rotate_extrude() intersection() {
                translate([.5, sqrt(2) / 2, 0]) circle(1);
                square([pivot / 2+1 - sqrt(2) / 2+2, sqrt(2)]);
            }
        }
    } // end contact points
} // end snap rings and end of model
```

THINKING ABOUT THESE MODELS: LEARNING LIKE A MAKER

In this book, we always talk a bit about the trial-and-error process that led to the models in each chapter. We think that makers may learn more from what did not work than from what did, and so we like to report our often-twisted path to each set of models.

The models in this chapter proved to be very difficult to develop, largely because the demonstrations are easier to work with if the models are bigger. However, we were trying to preserve some of the more interesting pendulum behavior in a small package so that they would work even on the smaller-end consumer 3D printers. If you have access to a bigger printer, you may want print the models from this chapter larger. If you do increase the size, do it with the appropriate parameters in the models, rather than by scaling up the STL. Not everything scales in a straightforward way.

The other issue with the last two models is that a smoothly functioning pivot is very important. In the case of the compound pendulum, the pivot is printed captive—that is, you will not be able to see it easily. You may need to work it around a little. Our first attempts had so much friction that the pendulum creaked once and stopped. Tweaking the parameters a bit fixed that for the compound pendulum.

The double pendulum was harder in part because two joints needed to move smoothly. For this case, we went with a simpler design—just a peg through a hole as the pivot—and added the small snap rings to keep the pieces from coming apart. This has the benefit that the arms can be printed separately and then assembled, though the conical contacts of the compound pendulum should give higher precision and lower friction (after a suitable amount of wear-in, at least). We also needed the arms in the double pendulum to be able to swing in a full 360-degree arc, which was not possible with the conical contact points.

Where to Learn More

Any good college-level introductory physics textbook will have a long discussion on pendulums. We used Joan's well-worn undergraduate copy of Halliday and Resnick's classic *Physics, Part 1, Third Edition* (Wiley, 1977), but there are more recent texts around that cover the material; the cited text appears to now be in its tenth edition. The chapter in any physics text will likely be called "Simple Harmonic Motion" or "Oscillations."

Wikipedia has a page on simple harmonic motion in general (https://en.wikipedia.org/wiki/Simple_harmonic_motion) and another on pendulums more specifically (https://en.wikipedia.org/wiki/Pendulum).

Applications of pendulums might also be interesting jumping-off points for student projects. The equation for the period of a simple pendulum can also be solved for *g*, Earth's gravitational constant, if you know the period of a pendulum and its length very accurately.

Teaching with These Models

Pendulums are usually first approached in depth at the AP or college level, because understanding the forces involved requires at least some fluency with trigonometry and (for the compound pendulum) basic calculus concepts. However, these models could also be used qualitatively to talk about forces and interactions, perhaps as discussed in www.nextgenscience.org/topic-arrangement/msforces-and-interactions or more generally to talk about scientific inquiry. The fact that the mass of the pendulum drops out of some of the calculations might lead to a discussion of dependencies.

If you are teaching this at the college level or just playing with it on your own, note that we designed the simple pendulum model to be easy to use for quickly creating pendulum demonstrations without needing to tape coins together. The complex and double pendulums work well enough for simple classroom demonstrations and could be used to talk about how to make a bigger and better one with more equipment.

Project Ideas

To get beyond the basic designs in this chapter you might want to think about some applications of pendlums. There are some classic ones to explore, notably the use of pendulums in clocks from Huygens's time to the present. There are designs on www.thingiverse.com for 3D printed clock mechanisms (search for "mechanical clock"), although these are complex prints that we have not been brave enough to try ourselves.

Depending on what resources you have, you might also think about trying to measure gravity successively more accurately. The first way to do it, as we described earlier, would be to just measure the pendulum length and period and derive an approximation from that. A Kater's pendulum (https://en.wikipedia.org/wiki/Kater's_pendulum) is a more sophisticated apparatus. Other pendulum gravimeters came later, which you might want to explore and perhaps approximate. These days, gravity departures from an Earth ideal value are measured by spacecraft, like the NASA GRACE mission (http://grace.jpl.nasa.gov/mission/gravity-101/).

If you have the ability to suspend a pendulum from a high place (in an atrium, perhaps) you could also try creating a Foucault pendulum (https://en.wikipedia.org/wiki/Foucault_pendulum), which is often seen in museums. Usually Foucault pendulums have a very long period (and thus a long string) and some means of marking the floor under them. As the earth turns, the swing of the pendulum gradually turns too, and it is possible to figure out your latitude from the pattern it makes.

The Foucault pendulum has to have a very long period so that it will move slowly enough that air resistance will not stop it before you see the effect. The bob needs to be heavy to minimize secondary effects like drafts that might mask the Earth rotation effects. In short, building one is pretty tricky, as the Wikipedia article describes.

Summary

This chapter describes how to 3D print three types of pendulum: a simple one to hang from a string; a compound (or physical) pendulum to pivot on a fulcrum; and a double pendulum, to demonstrate chaotic behavior. The chapter goes over some of the underlying physics and gives the equations for the period of the simple and compound pendulums. Finally, it talks about some of the limitations of the models and ways to branch out and create more sophisticated takes on these concepts.

CHAPTER 2

■ ■ ■

Geology

Geology is the study of how Earth evolves over time including how it was formed, what it is made of, and the changes that take place in it and on it. The term can be applied to other planets too, although sometimes that is called *planetary geology* or *astrogeology* to make the distinction. Whatever you elect to call it, geologic phenomena are complex and rarely have very simple mathematical models. We have picked a few surface feature types that we think are interesting and that can be hard to visualize without some sort of physical model.

In the first section, we talk about the process of *folding*. This process occurs when sediments build up over time and create layered rocks. Then compressive forces in the rocks may squash the sides of a set of layers and make them accordion up to create *synclines* (U-shaped bends) or *anticlines* (upward bumps). This is most extreme along tectonic plate boundaries, where big parts of the Earth's surface come together (for example, in the western United States). However, more spread-out folds can be found in the middle of plates, too, or may have been uplifted in the distant past (as is the case in the southern end of England and Wales).

Our model allows you to pick some parameters of the original layered sediment and change how and in which direction it bends to help you visualize different interesting structures, such as the ones that are often revealed in areas as widely distributed as road cuts in the American Southwest and chalk cliffs in the south of Britain.

The second model in this chapter explores sand dunes. *Dunes* are piles of sand that typically migrate along in the direction of the prevaling wind, gradually marching across sandy areas in long waves or trains. We particularly look at *barchan* dunes, crescent-shaped dunes that march across deserts (on Earth, Mars, and possibly Saturn's moon Titan) in long chains.

The phenomena in this chapter are complicated and impossible to model in full with a few pages of OpenSCAD. These models are designed so that if you have the dimensions of an actual phenomenon, you can create a 3D print starting there and vary the parameters to explore other scenarios for yourself or your students. Or if you just want to make a typical model for discussion purposes, you can use the values in the examples in this chapter.

© Joan Horvath and Rich Cameron 2017
J. Horvath and R. Cameron, *3D Printed Science Projects Volume 2*,
DOI 10.1007/978-1-4842-2695-7_2

Synclines and Anticlines

Sedimentary rock is built up by gradual deposition of silt or dust by water or wind. Sedimentary rocks develop a layered look as the rock being deposited varies over time. After the rock layers are laid down, that may not be the end of the story. In many parts of the world, particularly near the edges of tectonic plates, layers of rock may be squashed on the side, making them flex up or down. Even in the middle of a plate, the rocks might be gently squashed just a little. In either case, ripples start to appear in these layered rocks. If a ripple pokes up to make a bump, the ripple is called an *anticline* (Figure 2-1). If it loops downward to create an underground U-shape, it is called a *syncline* (Figure 2-2).

Figure 2-1. *Madison limestone in anticline in Sheep Mountain Canyon, Big Horn County, Wyoming, 1914. Courtesy of U.S. Geological Survey, Department of the Interior/USGS, www.sciencebase.gov/catalog/item/51dd7db8e4b0f72b4471b201*

Figure 2-2. *Syncline of black and gray banded slate at West Castleton, Rutland County, Vermont, 1900. Courtesy of U.S. Geological Survey, Department of the Interior/USGS,* www.sciencebase.gov/catalog/item/51dc3902e4b0f81004b7a61a

When rock layers are bent upward in an anticline, the oldest layers are pushed upward the most relative to where they would have been if there were no bending. If you imagine the curves on the hillside in Figure 2-1 getting steeper, you can imagine the oldest (deepest) layers getting squished upward more and more.

People searching for oil are interested in the existence of anticlines, because petroleum or natural gas can be squeezed out of the rock when anticlines are formed and fill a pocket at the uppermost part of anticline folds under the surface. Conversely, in a syncline, the deepest layers will tend to stay the deepest in the center of the bend, so they are less interesting to those hoping to find petrochemicals as near the surface as possible.

■ **Note**   A syncline or anticline might not be visible from the surface. The upward bump of an anticline might lie under many layers of other rocks and soil, and the surface above either formation might be perfectly flat.

Historical Context

One of the earliest mappings of synclines and anticlines was William Smith's 1815 geological map of England, later known as "The Map That Changed the World." It allowed analysis of how different types of rock may appear to be jumbled up, but might be reconstructed if one assumed that there were original layers built up at various times which were then folded and otherwise disrupted.

Smith carefully mapped how different fossils tended to be associated with particular layers, which allowed him to unravel a timeline of when various fossilized creatures were alive. This was not always obvious when layers were bent and twisted around in ways that could result in newer fossils being buried farther under the surface than earlier ones. This work laid the foundation for the evolutionists who came later to develop their theories.

■ **Note**   Author Simon Winchester has written a book about Smith and his times: ***The Map That Changed the World*** (Harper Collins, 2001). Smith did not receive recognition until late in his life, after episodes of having his work plagiarized and spending time in debtor's prison. You can also see Smith's map and read about him at `https://en.wikipedia.org/wiki/William_Smith_(geologist)`.

Printing an Anticline

It is easy to lose track of the three-dimensional geometry in a syncline or anticline formation if you are trying to visualize it in your head. As you may have discovered just by trying to follow along so far, it can be challenging to explain what it looks like to have a formation at an angle under a surface that might itself be at a different angle to the vertical. We hope our 3D-printable model will be a good tool for envisioning possible underground formations.

Creating a model of the forces under the Earth's surface that can bend rocks is more than we can do in a few-page OpenSCAD model. Instead, we have created a parameterized model that allows you to select values for the following (the model follows in Listing 2-1):

- A one-variable equation $y = f(x)$ for the shape of the **middle** layer of the model. In most cases this will be a sinusoid (see examples that follow). Note that the layers are created with their cross-sections in the x-y plane and extruded into the z direction. Layers are printed vertically for better resolution and to avoid support.

- How many layers the formation has, how thick each layer is, and the offset of a layer boundary from a baseline curve (negative offsets for below the curve, positive for above).

- A set of three numbers, layer_angle, which sets the angle (in degrees, x, y, and z) to rotate the layers once they have been created. The y-axis is perpendicular to the layers before they are rotated.

- Another set of three numbers, surface_angle (in degrees, *x*, *y*, and *z*) defining how to slice off part of the top surface relative to the base of the model, to mimic erosion or other forces that slice off some of the top of a formation. Figures 2-3, 2-4, and 2-5, respectively, show a single layer "formation" (light-colored object) rotated about the *x*, *y*, and *z* axis in turn by surface_angle. The model defines a box (the translucent pink box visible in Figures 2-3, 2-4, and 2-5), which is tilted at surface_angle and then intersected with the set of layers. Anything outside that box is cut off. We have kept a few lines of the model above each preview to show how these change relative to each other. The full listing (of a more complex multi-layer formation) is in Listing 2-1.

- Notice that the layers are first rotated through layer_angle and then cut off by the intersection of the box tilted at surface_angle. If this is too confusing, you might just experiment with different combinations one at a time to see the result in OpenSCAD's preview mode.

- A flag, include_layers, which determines whether to print the odd-numbered layers, even-numbered ones, all the layers, or an arbitrary set of layers. This allows for printing different layers in different colors if desired, as we have in this chapter.

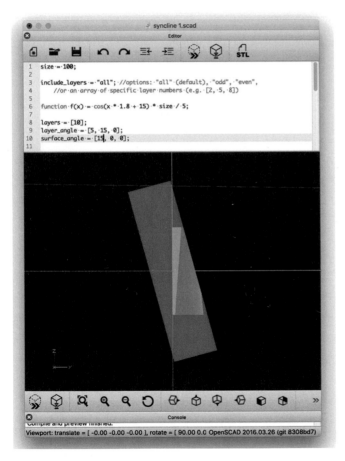

Figure 2-3. *A single layer function rotated only about the x-axis. View is of the y-z plane.*

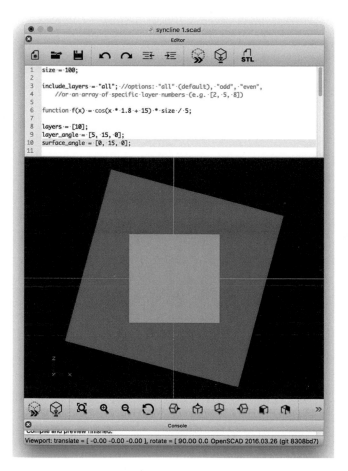

Figure 2-4. *A single layer function rotated only about the y-axis. View is of the x-z plane (looking at the side of the layer, so cosine function is not visible).*

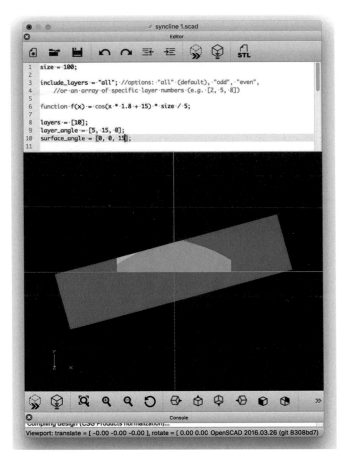

Figure 2-5. *A single layer function rotated only about the z-axis. View is of the x-y plane.*

■ **Note** Geologists like to think in terms of ***dip*** and ***dip direction***. ***Dip direction*** is represented in our model as the ***y*** value of the ***layer_angle*** variable if the ***z*** value is zero. ***Dip*** is the angle that the layer dips down relative to a horizontal surface. In our model this is the ***x*** value of the ***layer_angle*** variable, again if the ***z*** value is zero. There are good illustrations and a detailed description at https://en.wikipedia.org/wiki/Strike_and_ dip. (There is another convention for orientation, ***strike*** and ***dip***, which is less convenient for this model.) No component of surface_angle or layer_angle should exceed about 20 degrees to avoid printing issues.

Listing 2-1 creates an anticline with the surface layer partially "eroded" away (using the surface_angle variable) to make some of the layers visible (Figure 2-6). We show how to change the model to create a syncline in the next section of this chapter.

Figure 2-6. *Anticline model—printed in two sets, one odd and one even*

■ **Tip** The models will not stay together very well just by stacking them. We folded blue masking tape back on itself to create little tubes, sticky side out, and stuck those between the layers. It is also easy to put the layers together incorrectly; be sure to keep track of the order of the pieces and which way around they go. If you forget, remember that the top and bottom surfaces of a print (in the orientation that they were printed) are usually easy to distinguish from one another.

Listing 2-1. OpenSCAD Anticline Model

```
// File anticline.scad
// An OpenSCAD model of synclines and anticlines
// The program defines a function for the middle layer and then
// Defines layer thicknesses and offsets from this middle.
// Rich "Whosawhatsis" Cameron, November 2016
// Units: lengths in mm, angles in degrees, per OpenSCAD conventions
```

```
size = 100; //The dimension of the model in x and y, in mm

include_layers = "all"; //options: "all", "odd", "even",
                                    //or an array of specific layer
numbers (e.g. [2, 5, 8])

// Function that defines shape of center curve
function f(x) = cos(x * 1.5 + 30) * size / 5;

// offset of layer boundaries, relative to center curve
layers = [-20, -10, -6, 2, 10, 14, 22];
// Thickness of each layer = difference between subsequent offsets

layer_angle = [5, 15, 0];
// Vector of angles [x, y, z] rotating the curve relative to axes

surface_angle = [10, 0, 0];
// Vecto of angles about [x, y, z] to create sloping surface (top)
// Use to expose lower layers

// First create list of which layers to render
// (odd, even, all, or specific ones)
for(i = [0:len(layers) - 1]) if(
        ((include_layers == "odd") && (i % 2))
    ||
        ((include_layers == "even") && !(i % 2))
    ||
        (include_layers == "all")
    ||
        len(search(i, include_layers))
) translate([0, i*5, 0]) intersection() {

// Now create the layers and rotate them appropriately
// And intersect them with two bounding boxes defined below
// To cut off a clean flat bottom surface

    translate([-size / 2, 0, -size / 2]) cube([size, size, size]);
    rotate(surface_angle)
        cube([size * 2, size * .5, size * 2], center = true);
    rotate(layer_angle) linear_extrude(
        height = size * 2,
        center = true,
        convexity = 10
    ) {
        difference() {
            offset(layers[i]) layer();
            if(i) offset(layers[i - 1] + .2) layer();
        }
    }
}
```

```
//Function to make polygons out of curves
module layer() polygon(concat([
    for(i = [-size:size]) [i, f(i)]],
    [[size, -size],
    [-size, -size]
]));
//End model
```

Printing a Syncline

Listing 2-1 creates the anticline shown in Figure 2-6. To create a syncline, we changed some of the parameters and also decided to make the models a little smaller (by changing the size parameter) because we found the models were taking a long time. Note that simply scaling the whole model is tricky because the layers might get too thin. You really need to think through the parameters to change. The changes to Listing 2-1 are the following:

```
size = 80;
function f(x) = -cos(x * 1.8 + 15) * size / 5 + 30;
layers = [-22, -10, -3, 5, 13, 22];
layer_angle = [5, 15, 0];
surface_angle = [12, 0, 0];
```

The resulting syncline is shown in Figure 2-7. Notice that this is not just the negative of the anticline function. The model is created by first creating the layers, rotating them if applicable, and then intersecting the model with a cube to cut off a flat bottom surface. Given that *f(x)* would go negative without the +30 term, the result of this operation would be that there would be very little left, as you can see in the OpenSCAD screenshot in Figure 2-8. (The model gives an exploded view of the layers. You can see that many of the layers would just be little unprintable scraps.)

33

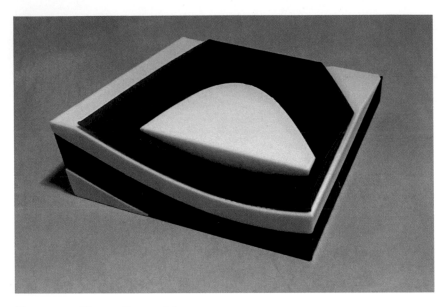

Figure 2-7. *The syncline model*

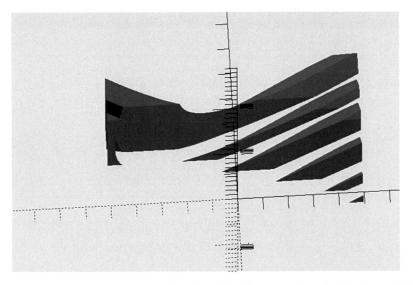

Figure 2-8. *The syncline model without the offset term, visualized in OpenSCAD*

Printing Tips for Syncline/Anticline Models

This model requires some degree of trial and error. Usually we try to have our prints be fairly foolproof, but in this case unless you use our examples as-is, you will need to look carefully at the pieces to be printed to be sure that they are not too small to be printed, too weirdly shaped, or not attached to the platform. Figures 2-9 and 2-10 show the odd and even pieces for the syncline model.

Figure 2-9. *Half of the syncline model in Figure 2-5 on the printer*

Figure 2-10. *The other half of the syncline model*

We recommend using a brim with these prints. A **brim** is a few loops on the platform around the base of a model, like the brim of a hat, which helps the model stick to the platform. You can see one in Figure 2-9. In some software, it may be called a "skirt" that is zero distance from the object.

■ **Tip**   In some circumstances you may want to use your printer program's "ungroup" capability to turn one or more of the pieces to a more printable direction. In some cases, in the output STL from OpenSCAD, pieces may be suspended in mid-air. They will need to be brought down to the 3D printer's platform and likely reoriented (180 degrees around the **y**-axis) in the program that you use to set up a print job (such as MatterControl, Cura, Repetier Host, or Makerbot Desktop).

In OpenSCAD, you may also want to add an offset term in the function **f(x)** to move the center layer up or down in the **y** direction as we do in the syncline model. Or you may use the surface_ angle or layer_angle parameters to get rid of small corner pieces by cutting off some of the upper surface. Using OpenSCAD's preview mode (see Appendix A) may be very helpful here.

The intent of this model is to help you gain insight into what formations look like when they have been squeezed, twisted, and then cut off at varying angles. It is important to remember that there is no geology knowledge encoded here and that this is purely a geometrical model. You may see physically inaccurate results if, for example, you make the amplitude of $f(x)$ very much higher than we have it in our sample code or if you increase the frequency of the sinusoid represented by $f(x)$ significantly. You will get results, but whether they are printable or represent a plausible formation is not possible to know in general.

3D PRINTING TERRAIN

The other way to get 3D printed models of interesting geological formations is to create them from one of the digital elevation databases that are available. The program we are partial to is Terrain2STL, developed by Thatcher Chamberlain. It is free and available at `http://jthatch.com/Terrain2STL/`. The website says it is based on a database with a resolution of 90 meters per pixel at the equator.

If you want to get a bit more out there still, Chamberlain's site also has an equivalent program for the Moon at `http://jthatch.com/Moon2STL/`. The site states that the moon data has a bit under 2 km per pixel resolution at the Moon's equator.

Figure 2-11 shows a print of the Rogue Valley area near Ashland, Oregon, from Terrain2STL. The program allows a user to select a region and how much to zoom in, and also allows the user to specify the vertical exaggeration. We often print out a "you are here" map of an area when we do an event. We are always amazed at how excited people get by it, and how much more insight you can gain from one than you can from a paper topographic map.

Figure 2-11. *Oregon's Rogue Valley (around Ashland), vertical scale exaggerated about ten times*

Dunes

The models in the first section of this chapter were about geological formations that evolve very slowly, on time scales that make a human lifetime seem less than a blink. We will close this chapter with a model of far more ephemeral phenomena: sand dunes.

Sand dunes are piles of sand that form and re-form driven by the wind. Some types of dunes are stationary (forming around an outcropping of rock or some vegetation), but the ones we talk about here often migrate across long distances. In particular, **barchan dunes** often form large fields like the one shown in Figure 2-12. These dunes are crescent-shaped, with the nose of the dune pointed into the wind and long trailing horns on the downwind side. Wind would be blowing from the top of the picture towards the bottom in Figure 2-12. The darker areas are soil and plants between the dunes. These areas are lower than the dunes. Barchans typically form in "sand-starved" areas, where there is not enough sand for very deep seas of standing piles of sand to form.

Figure 2-12. *Compound barchan dune in a downwind area of the White Sands National Monument, New Mexico. Dunes and interdune spaces are of approximately equal extent (rotated 90 degrees from original). Courtesy of U.S. Geological Survey, Department of the Interior/USGS,* www.sciencebase.gov/catalog/item/51dd88f3e4b0f72b4471c140

Dunes start to form when wind piles up sand a bit, and this pile then has other sand blown up against it. The sand piles up steeply on the side facing into the wind (pushed by the wind). The side away from the wind slides down at the ***angle of repose***, the maximum angle that a pile of loose material can sustain in a stable way. Figure 2-13 shows the details of this crest, where the slope pushed up by the wind meets the lee slope where material will slide down at the angle of repose, creating a relatively sharp curved edge along the top of the dune. The entire dune will march across the desert, progressing like a single wave on the sea.

Figure 2-13. *White Sands National Monument, New Mexico. Crest of barchan dune (wind blowing from left to right). Photo by J.R. Douglass, U.S. National Park Service, 1964. Courtesy of U.S. Geological Survey, Department of the Interior/USGS,* www.sciencebase. gov/catalog/item/51dd894ee4b0f72b4471c19a

The Model

There are many mathematical models of the formation of sand dunes. Typically they model the statistical behavior of many sand grains to create a simulation of the flow of dunes across a space. The classic book in this field (originally published in 1941) is R. A. Bagnold's ***The Physics of Blown Sand and Desert Dunes*** (reissued by Courier Corporation, 2005). However, this was way beyond the scope of our book. As with the folded-rock models, we wanted to "3D surface fit" data to reproduce the basic shape of a dune while retaining as much of the physics as possible. Figure 2-14 shows the resulting 3D print.

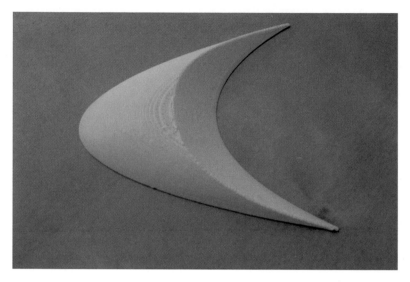

Figure 2-14. *Barchan dune model*

There are three different parabolic curves used to create the 3D surface fit of this model, shown in full in Listing 2-2. The base of the windward side of the dune (the left side in Figure 2-12) is modeled by the first parabola which depends on the variables `height`, `width`, and `length` of the dune. `length` is the distance along the centerline from nose to tips of the crescent, and `width` is the distance between the two tips of the crescent.

The second parabola is the symmetrical dune cross-section, the pink structures in Figures 2-15 and 2-16. The angle of the windward side to the horizontal (typicallly 15 degrees, according to Bagnold and other sources) is the variable `windward`, and the angle of repose is the variable `repose`, typically 30 degrees for sand. These cross-sections depend on the angle `windward` and the variable `height`. These are offset so that the one end of each cross-section falls along the first parabola that forms the windward edge. All these cross-sections are the same as each other and are not rotated to follow the windward edge parabola, as is clear in Figures 2-15 and 2-16.

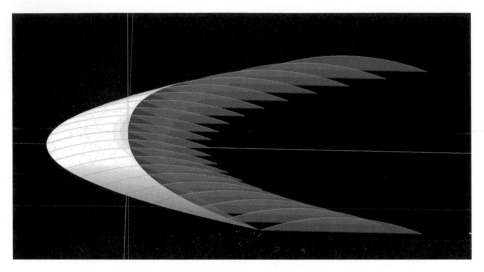

Figure 2-15. *Barchan dune model cross-sections (pink) lined up along the parabola that forms the windward base of the dune*

Figure 2-16. *The cross sections in 2-15 viewed from above*

To create the lee side, a set of rectangles (Figures 2-17 and 2-18) is generated along a third, leeward edge parabola. This leeward parabola is specified by all the same variables as the first parabola, plus the height and the two specified angles. Figure 2-18 shows these rectangles from above.

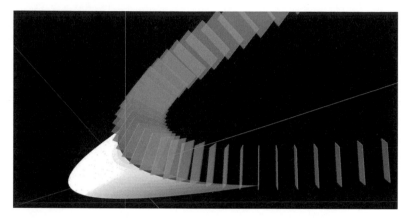

Figure 2-17. *The rectangles that define the lee face of the dune*

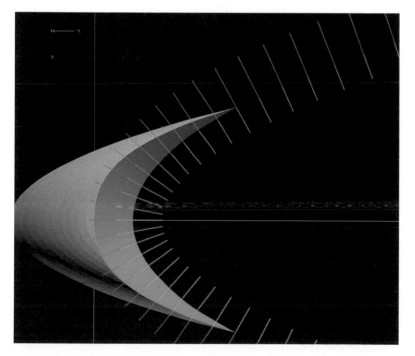

Figure 2-18. *The rectangles in 2-17 from above*

Finally, two surfaces are created using OpenSCAD's hull() function, one that will create the windward side and one that will be subtracted from the windward side to create the lee slope. Loosely speaking, the hull() function creates the smallest possible convex shape that includes all the points you ask the hull() function to combine. The first hull across the cross-sections creates the windward side. Then a second surface is created by using the hull() fuction on the rectangles forming the lee side. The lee side is then subtracted from the windward side to give the final dune shape.

Printing the Dune Model

The barchan dune model is easy to print for just about any reasonable value of angle of repose and windward angle. It should not be necessary to use support or a brim—after all, the shape can be generated by wind blowing around sand, so the dunes are "additively manufactured" in real life.

■ **Caution**   This model takes a while to render in OpenSCAD—you may need to leave it running for a while before your model appears. See Appendix A (or the OpenSCAD manual) for how to use "preview" instead of full rendering.

Listing 2-2. Barchan Dune OpenSCAD Model

```
// File barchan.scad
// An OpenSCAD model of barchan sand dunes
// The program defines a parabola for the envelope
// Based on the parameters at the top of the file.
// Rich "Whosawhatsis" Cameron, November 2016
// Units: lengths in mm, angles in degrees, per OpenSCAD conventions

height = 10; // max height in z, mm
windward = 15; // angle to the horizontal of the nose of the dune
repose = 30; // angle of repose, degrees
width = 100; // width at widest point (ends of crescent), mm
length = 100; // length from nose to center of crescent ends, mm

// First create cross sections of the dune in the vertical plane
// parallel to the wind direction
// These cross sections are offset by a parabola
// The back of the cross section, defined by angle of repose
// for now, is symmetrical to the front
// Later on we will subtract (difference) a cutoff at the angle of
// repose

difference() {
    for(i = [-width/2:width/2 - 1])
        hull() for(i = [i, i + 1])
```

```
        translate([i, pow(i/width * 2, 2) * length, 0])
            rotate([90, 0, 90])
                linear_extrude(height = .001, scale = .001)
                    polygon([
                        for(i = [-1:.1:1])
                            height * [i / tan(windward), 1 - i * i]
                    ]);

    // The next section creates the surface that we will subtract
    // from the windward side to create the angle of repose
    // on the leeward side
    hull() for(i = [-width:width]) {
        translate([
            i,
            height / tan(repose) + (length - height / tan(repose) -
                height / tan(windward)) / pow(width / 2, 2) * pow(i, 2),
            0
        ]) {
            rotate([
                90,
                0,
                90 + atan(2 * i * (length - height / tan(repose) -
                    height / tan(windward)) / pow(width / 2, 2))
// The previous line calculates the normal to the lee face parabola.
            ]) {
                linear_extrude(height = .001, scale = 1) {
                    rotate(90 - repose) translate([0, -1, 0]) square((height + 2)
                    / sin(repose));
                } // end linear_extrude
            } // end rotate
        } // end translate
    } // end hull
} // end difference
// (subtracting the leeward face cutout from the rest of the model)
```

Barchan Dunes Beyond Earth

Barchan dunes have been spotted elsewhere in the solar system including on Mars and on Saturn's moon Titan. Figure 2-19 shows these dunes on Mars. On Mars, though, the mechanism is a little different than on Earth, and thus the shape is different. Some scientists postulate that the dunes are stretched out because they are partially frozen some of the year, and the frozen nose of the dune does not move the way one would expect a dune on Earth to migrate, so the dune stretches out in one dimension or another. V. Schatz, H. Tsoar, K. S. Edgett, E. J. R. Parteli, and H. J. Herrmann postulated this in their *Journal of Geophysical Research* paper, "Evidence for indurated sand dunes in the Martian north polar region," 28 April 2006.

Figure 2-19. *Image of barchan dunes on Mars from the High Resolution Imaging Science Experiment (HiRISE) on the Mars Reconnaisance Orbiter. Distance between the two horns of the merging dune is a bit over 500 meters. NASA/JPL/University of Arizona,* www.uahirise.org/ESP_014404_1765

Not a lot is known about dunes on other worlds yet. There is not yet enough data, for example, to know whether barchan dunes on Mars migrate. There are also conflicting opinions in the scientific literature about the correct angle of repose to use. HiRISE scientist Nathan Bridges wrote a summary of aeolian processes on Mars and Titan that is a good snapshot of ongoing research: www.planetary.org/blogs/guest-blogs/2015/0326-lpsc-2015-aeolian-processes-mars-titan.html.

■ **Note**   Because the shape of a barchan dune on Mars and Titan is so much different from that of one on Earth, the model we have created for Earth dunes does not readily change to support the extraterrestrial versions.

THINKING ABOUT THESE MODELS: LEARNING LIKE A MAKER

It always seems to be true that our models wind up being far more complex than we expect them to be, and this chapter was no exception. We thought the syncline/anticline model would be relatively easy—just define a basic curve and offset layers on either side. As with the real geology, the geometry quickly gets complex and can create layers that are difficult if not impossible to print because they are very thin, are curved on the default bottom side, or perhaps are in mid-air. It also turned out to be harder to explain what the model was doing than to write it in the first place!

We try to make all our models easy to print on consumer printers, and the examples we give in the chapter should print reasonably reliably. However, if you start to change the layers and angling to mimic a real formation, you may create a layer that is too thin. Preview your model carefully (in OpenSCAD or your printer's slicing software) before committing to a print.

In the case of the sand dunes, we were surprised at how difficult it was to find an empirical, simple model in terms of a few equations. Most of the models we found were complex physics simulations modeling the movement of sand grains (a process called **saltation**). Rich started off modeling the base shape as an ellipse and then tried creating and scaling cross-sections along a parabola, before realizing that the nose and lee face needed to be generated with separate functions because they are governed by different forces.

In the end Rich created a three-dimensional surface fit to Earth barchan dunes. Unfortunately, because it *is* a carefully tuned set of curve fits, it cannot generate the shapes of barchan dunes on other planets based on changes to embedded physics models. However, we suggest this extension of the model as a project to consider doing yourself!

Where to Learn More

The topics in this chapter would commonly be taught in an undergraduate class in physical geology. Our go-to reference was the textbook by W. K. Hamblin and E. H. Christiansen, *Earth's Dynamic Systems*, 9th Edition (Prentice-Hall, 2001). If you want more easy-to-interpret sketches about geological formations, you may like David Lambert and the Diagram Group's book *The Field Guide to Geology* (Facts on File, 1998).

The U.S. Geological Survey's education site (http://education.usgs.gov) has fact sheets and links to resources at a variety of different levels. The U.S. National Park Service also has resources online about the geology of national parks; we enjoyed the writeup on types of dunes at www.nps.gov/grsa/learn/nature/dune-types.htm.

The geology of southern England is complex, and many fine examples can be found there of folded and uplifted rock. The Geological Society's website (`www.geolsoc.org.uk`) is another treasure trove of imagery and descriptions of interesting formations.

Barchan and other dune formations on other planets are mostly described in the peer-reviewed scientific literature at this point, which can be heavy reading and may not be easily accessible. For example, possible barchans on Saturn's moon Titan are described in a *Nature Geoscience* paper by R. C. Ewing, A. G. Hayes, and A. Lucas, "Sand dune patterns on Titan controlled by long-term climate cycles," 8 December 2014. But if you search on the phrase "barchan dune," you can find examples and photos of dunes on Earth and beyond and descriptions of the various models for their dynamics. You can also search on "aeolian processes" to learn about related phenomena.

Teaching with These Models

The initial trigger for this chapter was Joan's husband (a British expat) musing about how nice it would have been to have had 3D printed models when he was studying geology of the south of England. It is complex to infer from the eroded surface what might lie beneath. The most straightforward way to use these models in education is to print a few that demonstrate the structure you are trying to study. One option might be to create a layered model of an underground or partially exposed formation and also print the terrain above it, as described in the sidebar "3D Printing Terrain."

If you are a K-12 teacher, 3D printed models might be appropriate companions to having students create syncline and anticline clay models, as shown on paleontologist Jim Lehane's site (`http://jazinator.blogspot.com/2010/05/teaching-folds-using-play-doh.html`). This site also has a lot of other links for K-12 teachers, including worksheets tied to movies that have incorrect depictions of geology. Teaching about Earth science standards, such as "Earth's Systems" (`www.nextgenscience.org/pe/ms-ess2-2-earths-systems`), might benefit from these models.

Project Ideas

The most obvious way to use the layered-rock models is to create one that mimics a real formation or create a hypothetical one for discussions. If you want to make an elaborate model, you can make it in sections, but you will have to think hard about how to change the function for the middle layer and any rotations.

The barchan model is a little bit more of a one-off curiousity, but you might play with some of the variables like the angle of repose and see how this model changes. Angle of repose is dependent on the properties of the sand or other granular materials, and the shape of the lee side of the dune will change because of this. Results should be taken with a grain of salt (or maybe sand?) because this model does not really capture the interactions between the windward and lee sides of the dune, other than making some simple geometrical assumptions.

You can also think of the barchan as a case study of how to "surface fit" something based loosely on its physics plus its geometry, a situation that might come up more often than just in models of ephemeral sand phenomena.

Summary

This chapter shows how to create models of two types of geological formations. The first model allows you to create visualizations of layered rock formations similar to those found in many parts of the world where sedimentary rock is compressed and squeezed or uplifted. The second model is a 3D surface fit of a barchan dune, a particular type of dune that occurs in areas without a lot of sand. The model is tuned for barchan dunes on Earth, but these dunes are also found on Mars and possibly on Saturn's moon Titan. The chapter also notes other available software for printing terrain and some ways to use the models.

CHAPTER 3

■ ■ ■

Snow and Ice

Water has some pretty weird properties. For example, it expands as it freezes; most other substances contract as they freeze. In this chapter we talk about ice and snow and create models of some of the more intriguing geometries that frozen water can create.

Water Ice

Figure 3-1 shows a familiar sight: an ice cube floating in water. The density of ice is 0.9167 grams per cubic centimeter at the freezing point; water at the same temperature is 0.9998 grams per cubic centimeter. If you add salt to the water (as we did in the cup of water in Figure 3-1), the saltwater becomes even denser. To make it roughly the same as seawater, add about a teaspoon and a half of table salt (8 grams) to 1 cup of water (https://en.wikipedia.org/wiki/Salt).

Figure 3-1. *Fresh water ice in salt water*

© Joan Horvath and Rich Cameron 2017
J. Horvath and R. Cameron, *3D Printed Science Projects Volume 2*,
DOI 10.1007/978-1-4842-2695-7_3

In the little experiment shown in Figure 3-1, a few drops of juice were added to the ice to make it more visible. Saltwater has a density of about 1.025 grams per cubic centimeter. We would expect about 10% of the volume of the ice to be above water in this case, because of the relative densities of ice and the liquid water it is floating in. Water expands as it freezes because it creates a crystal lattice of hexagons (Figure 3-2). Water molecules consist of two hydrogen atoms and an oxygen atom. When water freezes, each water molecule connects to four others in a roughly tetrahedral structure. In this chapter we explore the visible effects of that structure.

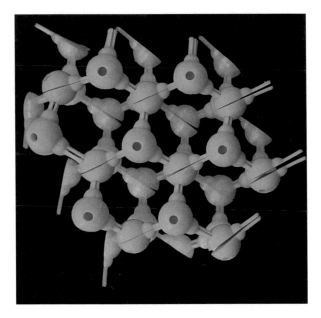

Figure 3-2. *Molecular structure of an ice crystal*

■ **Note**   We developed the 3D-printable, molecular-level model of ice crystals in Figure 3-2 in our previous **3D Printed Science Projects** book (Apress, 2016, Chapter 7, "Molecules"). The larger spheres represent oxygen atoms; the smaller half-spheres between these spheres, hydrogen atoms. Each molecule in the lattice is connected to four others. Each oxygen has two hydrogens and two holes for connecting other oxygen atoms' hydrogens. There are different ways the atoms can be connected to each other in hexagons. This one is called **ice 1c**.

Icebergs

Among the more intriguing results of the properties of freezing water are ***icebergs***, giant floating mountains of ice. Typically they ***calve*** (split off) from glaciers to be carried around by currents until eventually they melt and erode away. Because they come from glaciers on land, fed by snow, icebergs are made of freshwater, not frozen ocean water. This fact has led some to suggest towing them to parched regions, like Southern California or Saudi Arabia, but as of this writing no one has pulled that off.

The fact that ice is 10% lighter than an equal volume of liquid water means that icebergs are about 90% submerged. As noted earlier in the chapter, seawater is a little denser still than freshwater, and makes a small additional difference (about 3.5% for the saltwater we created at the beginning of the chapter).

Icebergs represent famous hazards to navigation; the best-known example is the sinking of the ***Titanic*** when it struck an iceberg on its maiden voyage in 1912. Icebergs can pitch over, roll, or oscillate as they melt or as pieces break off and become unstable, which can be an even more serious hazard to any nearby ships. You can see this for yourself in a spectacular YouTube video from the Weather Channel at `https://youtu.be/mvQ4eDKf9UY`, or search YouTube for "rolling iceberg."

Tabular icebergs split off from glaciers as thick slabs of ice, often with some less-compacted snow on top. Some of these icebergs can be huge. Iceberg B-15 calved from the Ross Ice Shelf in Antarctica in March 2000. It was 295 kilometers by 37 kilometres wide; recognizable pieces of it were detected for five years. By the time you read this, the Larsen C Ice Shelf in Antartica may have split along a deep rift that formed in 2016 and created an iceberg that, temporarily at least, will be about half the size of B-15.

The Model

We have developed a model of a tabular iceberg to visualize the above-water and below-water sections of an iceberg. Because icebergs come in all sorts of shapes and sizes, we decided to create two different sample models: one that is fundamentally a cylinder (with a variable radius) and another that is a ***frustrum*** of a cone (a cone with the top cut off).

Cylindrical Iceberg

Our first iceberg model is a cylinder, modified to have a variable radius. It is shown in Figure 3-3. The fine line near the top is the waterline (90% of the volume). In the open ocean, the part above that line would be the only part visible. The model allows you to set the height and the radius and to change the parameters `featuresize`, `noise`, and `smoothness` to respectively change how big the departures from a circle are, how many of them there are, and how much they have been smoothed out. Then the model extrudes this wavy-circle base straight up into a wavy cylinder. The model is given in Listing 3-1.

Figure 3-3. *Cylindrical iceberg, with 10% volume line near top*

Listing 3-1. The Cylindrical Iceberg

```
// File CylindricalIceberg.scad
// An OpenSCAD model of an iceberg
// Rich "Whosawhatsis" Cameron, January 2017
height = 30; // height overall, in mm
radius = 40; // maximum radius
featuresize = 20; // maximum variation from of radius
noise = 10; // frequency of variations in radius
smoothness = 2; // how much to smooth the variations
seed = 0; // seed for random number generator
linedepth = .2; // should be about half of your nozzle diameter

percentDistance = .9; // location of the water line

$fs = .5;
$fa = 2;

// extrude the wavy outline and subtract the water line
difference() {
    union() {
        linear_extrude(height, convexity = 5) outline();
        if(linedepth < 0)
            translate([0, 0, height * percentDistance])
```

```
            linear_extrude(.5, center=true, convexity=5)
                offset(-linedepth) outline();
    }
    if(linedepth>0)
        translate([0, 0, height * percentDistance])
            linear_extrude(.5, center=true, convexity=5)
                difference() {
                    offset (2) outline();
                    offset(-linedepth) outline();
                }
}

module outline() offset(-smoothness) offset(smoothness * 2)
    offset(-smoothness) polygon([for(
        theta=[0:noise:359],
        r=rands(radius, radius - featuresize, 1, seed+theta)
    ) rect(r, theta)]);

function rect(r, theta)=r * [sin(theta), cos(theta)];

// End of model
```

Frustrum Iceberg

For our second model, we based our shape on the frustrum of a cone (a cone with the top cut off). As with the cylinder, we made the radius of the cone vary randomly. To solve this in general is very complicated. As is often the case for engineering problems, you can often vastly simplify things by changing just one of many parameters. In this case, we fixed the ratio of the size of the top of the iceberg to the bottom.

Even with this simplification, though, it takes a bit of geometry to figure out where the line of 10% volume falls. Figure 3-4 shows how we set up the problem. The blue (bottom) frustrum of the cone is in two parts: one that is 10% of the volume (on top) and one that is 90% (which will be below water in the real thing).

To make the math relatively tidy, we made a simplifying assumption that the frustrum was half the volume of a cone that includes the red (top) cone and the blue (bottom) frustrum, or a cone of height c in Figure 3-4. In other words, the red (top) cone is a cone that has the same volume as the blue frustrum.

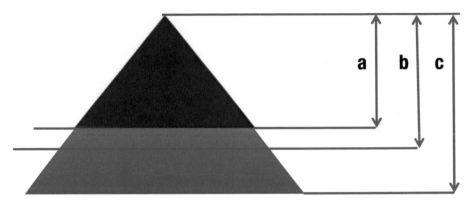

Figure 3-4. *The geometry of the frustrum iceberg model*

It turns out that by thinking of the cones of height ***a***, ***b***, and ***c*** as all being similar (having the same angle at the top), you can show yourself that the volume of the cone of heights ***a***, ***b***, and ***c*** vary by the cube root of the height, because the radius will vary linearly with the height, and the area of the base goes as the square of the radius.

We know that the volume of a cone is one-third the area of the base times the height. So if we want to have the volume of the cone of height ***c*** be twice that of the red (top) cone, ***c*** will have to equal the cube root of 2 (which is about 1.2599) times the height ***a***.

For the frustrum section between ***a*** and ***b*** to be 10% of the volume between lines ***a*** and ***c***, ***b*** has to be the cube root of 1.1 (which is 1.0322) times ***a***. The red (top) cone is just a convenience to help think about the geometry. All we want is the percentage difference between ***b*** and ***c*** so we know where the waterline is. Because we "throw away" the upper cone, we can have arbitrary values for the height and width of the frustrum, and the relationship will still hold. We will want the 10% line, then, to be at ***(c – b) / (c – a)***, or (1.2599 – 1.0322) / (1.2599 – 1) = 87.6% of the way from the bottom to the top.

Finally, based on Cavalieri's Principle (`https://en.wikipedia.org/wiki/Cavalieri's_principle`), we can argue that as long as the curve we use for the base is extruded consistently from bottom to top, this holds for our wavy frustrum too. The result of all that math is shown in Figure 3-5 and the OpenSCAD model in Listing 3-2. The indented line would be the water line (at height ***b*** in Figure 3-4).

Figure 3-5. *The frustrum iceberg model on a 3D printer*

Listing 3-2. The Frustrum Iceberg Model

```
// File FrustrumIceberg.scad
// An OpenSCAD model of an iceberg
// Rich "Whosawhatsis" Cameron, January 2017
height = 30; // height overall, in mm
radius = 40; // maximum radius
featuresize = 20; // maximum variation from of radius
noise = 10; // frequency of variations in radius
smoothness = 2; // how much to smooth the variations
seed = 0; // seed for random number generator
linedepth = .2; // should be about half of your nozzle diameter

CRRadius = pow(1.1, 1/3); //cube root of 1.1
CR2 = pow (2, 1/3); // cube root of 2
// calculate the location of the water line
percentDistance = (CR2 - CRRadius) / (CR2 -1);
topScale = 1/CR2; // scale of top of frustrum relative to base

$fs = .5;
$fa = 2;
```

```
// extrude the wavy outline with the top scalled and
// subtract the water line at the height calculated above
difference() {
    union() {
        linear_extrude(height, scale=topScale, convexity=5)
            outline();
        if(linedepth<0) intersection() {
            translate([0, 0, height * percentDistance])
                cube(
                    [radius * 10, radius * 10, .5],
                    center=true
                );
            linear_extrude(height, scale=topScale, convexity=5)
                offset(-linedepth) outline();
        }
    }
    if(linedepth>0) intersection() {
        translate([0, 0, height * percentDistance])
            cube([radius * 10, radius * 10, .5], center=true);
        linear_extrude(height, scale=topScale, convexity=5)
            difference() {
                offset(2) outline();
                offset(-linedepth) outline();
            }
    }
}

module outline() offset(-smoothness) offset(smoothness * 2)
    offset(-smoothness) polygon([for(
        theta=[0:noise:359],
        r=rands(radius, radius - featuresize, 1, seed+theta)
    ) rect(r, theta)]);

function rect(r, theta)=r * [sin(theta), cos(theta)];

// End of model
```

Printing and Changing the Model

The model allows you to set the height and the radius and to change the parameters featuresize, noise, and smoothness to respectively change how big the departures from a right circular cone are, how many of them there are, and whether they have been smoothed out.

Because the indentation is a delicate feature, you may need to play with different slicing settings or even programs for best results.

Floating the Iceberg

It is tempting to try to float the iceberg model. However, because your prints will not be solid, we cannot give you a guaranteed reproducable way to have the iceberg float at a particular percentage of its volume. However, here are some useful numbers in case you want to try to make it work: PLA (the commonest plastic used in consumer 3D printers) is around 1.25 grams per cubic centimeter.

A 3D print will require you to set a value for *infill* (what percentage of the print is filled in with plastic, versus the volume being left full of air). We printed ours at 20% infill. In addition, the boundary of the object is solid plastic—let's call that another 5%. Thus the average density of our print (air plus plastic) will be around 25% of 1.25, or 0.313. Water is just below 1 gram per cubic centimeter, as we noted earlier, so our print should be around 31% submerged. As you can see in Figure 3-6, it looks pretty close to that.

Figure 3-6. *The PLA iceberg afloat in tap water*

We can see that to get to 90% submerged we would have to go to 65% or so infill, plus the 5% perimeter, or 70% times the 1.25 density. That would eat a lot of time and filament, so you probably don't want to create an accurately floating iceberg this way. If your printer uses ABS, that material has a density of only 1.05 grams per cubic centimeter, so you would need to use about 85% or so infill to be 90% submerged.

Vase Printing

You can also *vase print* your model. This means that you print a base and sides, but no top. Many slicers have a "spiral vase" option, and most others can be explicitly configured to print 0% infill and 0 solid layers on top, which has a similar effect. In MatterControl (see Appendix A), this setting is under Settings ➤ General ➤ Single Print ➤ Spiral Vase (with a box to select).

If you have vase prints, you can experiment with filling them 90% full of water (Figure 3-7). They should ride just a bit below the surface because of the heavier PLA displacing a bit more water. If you fill them 90% full of water, that is equivalent to filling them full of ice. Don't try to freeze water in them, though, because the ice will likely break the PLA as it freezes and expands.

Figure 3-7. *The two vase-printed icebergs in water*

Snow

Water's peculiar structure has many other implications, too. Snow has many of the properties it does because of the way snowflakes build up as they move though clouds. Snowflakes are crystals, too, always with six sides because of ice's fundamental hexagonal structure. Creating an accurate model of snowflake formation is way beyond what we can sensibly do in this book. But we can come up with a simple model that you can then play with and see what structures result in the landscapes like the one in Figure 3-8.

Figure 3-8. *A snowy late winter afternoon in Boston*

Physics of Snowflakes

Snowflakes are additively manufactured in clouds, but unlike 3D prints, they are not built up one layer at a time. Instead they accrete material in ways that depend on the conditions the flake encounters as it forms. Material is added mostly around the flake's perimeter, rather than making the flake thicker. The temperature in the cloud and the excess water around at the time (called ***supersaturation***) are the major determiners of what type of snowflake you will get.

The Snow Crystal Morphology diagram — sometimes called the Nakaya diagram, for 1930s physicist Ukichiro Nakaya—lays out what kinds of snowflakes form at various combinations of supersaturation and temperature. The Tip that follows lists some resources to find the details.

■ **Tip**   California Institute of Technology researcher Kenneth Libbrecht's book ***Field Guide to Snowflakes*** (Voyageur Press preprint, 2016) was a valuable resource that helped us think about the snowflake models, along with his website `www.snowcrystals.com`. It features pictures of and discussions about the physics of 21 different structures. The snowflake entry in Wikipedia is good too: `https://en.wikipedia.org/wiki/Snowflake`.

Our model here focuses on ***dendrites***, the typical star-shaped snowflake form that you cut out of paper in third grade. These tend to form when the air is supersaturated and the temperatue is just below freezing (down to about –3.5 degrees Centigrade) or when the temperature is between –10 and –22 degrees Centigrade. Other than in those regimes, snowflakes can be solid plates or prisms, thick or thin, columns, and more, but always with the six-fold symmetry of the underlying crystal structure (except when two partially formed flakes merge).

■ **Note** There are many 3D-printable snowflake models. One of the most ambitious is the Snowflake Machine (`www.thingiverse.com/thing:1159436`) by Laura Taalman (a.k.a. Mathgrrl). This model (also in OpenSCAD) allows for many different variations of snowflakes with the Thingiverse Customizer.

The Model

The snowflakes we create here (like the one in Figure 3-9) will always be perfectly six-fold symmetrical (all six arms the same). Snowflakes in the wild are not always perfect, but we assume that here.

Figure 3-9. *Snowflake model*

The model (in Listing 3-3) works by creating randomly sized hexagonal pieces and accreting the smaller ones onto larger ones. The probability of the size and position of a given hexagonal addition is driven by OpenSCAD's random number generator modified by a power law. You can change the parameter `distribution` in Listing 3-3 so that the size distribution of the hexagons being added follows the functions for cube, fifth power, and so on. The flake in Figure 3-9 was created with the default values of all the parameters in Listing 3-3.

Listing 3-3. Snowflake Model

```
// File snowflake.scad
// An OpenSCAD model of an iceberg
// Rich "Whosawhatsis" Cameron, January 2017
// Units: lengths in mm, angles in degrees
// per OpenSCAD conventions

min = 2; // minimum size of a hexagon
// should be large enough to print without breaking
max = 12; // maximum size of a hexagon
distribution = 5; //exponent in power law
smooth = .5; // smooth off edges
// simulates snowflake, melting/sublimating a bit
seed = 10; // seed for random number generator
// same seed gives same result
iterations = 20; // how many times to add more hexagons
layer = 1; // how much smaller to make each layer than the last
minwidth = 0.5; // stops iterating branches if they get too
// thin to print, which would result in disconnected sections

$fs = .5;
$fa = 2;

// First create an array of random numbers skewed by power law
// Random number is raised to the power "distribution"
// and scaled by max-min
array = [
   for(v = rands(0, max - min, iterations, seed))
      min + pow(v, distribution) /
         pow(max - min, distribution - 1)
];

// Create six arms
for(i = [0:3]) linear_extrude(1+i * .5)
   offset(smooth) offset(-smooth * 2) offset(smooth)
      for(a = [0:60:359]) rotate(a) grow(shrink-i * layer);

// recursive function that grows each arm or branch
module grow(n = 1, branch = true, shrink = 0) {
   // create one hexagon
   circle(array[n] - shrink, $fn = 6);
   // then decide whether to continue with recursion
   if(n < len(array) && (array[n] - shrink) > minwidth) {
      translate([
         abs(array[n] - array[n+1])+1 - shrink,
         0,
         0
      ])
         grow(n+1, branch, shrink);
```

```
        // branch if size has decreased sufficiently
        if((array[n] - 2)>array[n+1] && n>5 && branch)
            for(a=[60, -60]) rotate(a)
                translate([abs(array[n] - array[n+1])+1, 0, 0])
                    grow(n+1, false, shrink+1);
    }
}
// End model
```

Printing and Changing the Model

The best way to explore the model is to play with the various parameters. The model creates hexagons with a random distribution of size, so the biggest effect can be changing the seed.This model can create dendrites and basic hexagonal shapes. Figure 3-10 shows some example flakes with a few parameters changed from the values in Listing 3-3. The one on the left has iterations = 10, making it stubbier and closer to a stellar plate type flake; the one in the middle has distribution = 10, seed = 3, and layer = *0.5*; and the one on the right has layer = 0.*5,* seed = 3, and distribution = 15.

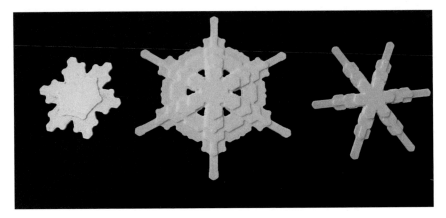

Figure 3-10. *Snowflakes with different parameters, as described in the text*

If you would like to make the more basic geometrical shapes (six-sided columns or prisms), Rich has posted a set of open source constant-geometry shapes on Youmagine that could get you started. You can find them at www.youmagine.com/designs/fixed-volume-objects.

```
┌─────────────────────────────────────────────────────┐
│       THINKING ABOUT THESE MODELS: LEARNING           │
│                    LIKE A MAKER                        │
└─────────────────────────────────────────────────────┘
```

As seems to be the case with many of these models, the most difficult part was justifying the correctness of our mathematics after an intuitive leap to an answer. We spent quite a bit of time finding a mathematical model for the iceberg that would actually hold water, so to speak, for different values of height and radius. We found that just hand drawing the problem a lot of different ways was invaluable. We initially were trying to solve an even more general version of the problem and realized that the simplification we use in the chapter would make it feasible to create a model that was not overly complicated.

For the snowflake, we wanted to keep the physics as accurate as possible. However, to really model what is going on with water accreting is very complex, so we compromised and created a simple but flexible model that allows the user to change the probability distribution (sort of) that the accreting snowflake uses. As we discuss in the section, we knew there were already good snowflake models out there. We wanted to create one that was very simple, had a reasonable physical basis, and could be a good platform for further explorations.

Where to Learn More

The study of Arctic snow and ice has taken on a particular urgency in the light of climate change, which might cause large ice sheets to collapse into icebergs. You can look up the history of Antarctic ice sheets Larsen A, B, and C. Larsen A and B collapsed in 1995 and 2002, respectively. As we write in early 2017, Larsen C seems to be headed for the same fate. There is a summary at https://en.wikipedia.org/wiki/Larsen_Ice_Shelf. This is relevant to people far from Antarctica, because if these large ice sheets float away from Antarctica and melt, sea levels may begin to rise significantly. Understanding how and why ice sheets calve into icebergs and how long it takes for them to melt will be a key scientific endeavor in the coming years.

For more about snowflakes, as noted earlier, the work of Caltech's Kenneth Libbrecht is a good and accessible source at the level of his general-public books and website already mentioned. He also has professional papers in this sphere, if you have access to scientific journals. Unfortunately, a lot of the math to fully simulate snowflake calculation is better suited to supercomputers—one has to bear in mind complicated interactions between the air, the forming snowflake, water vapor in the air, and so on. A good survey of current research can be found in Ron Cowan's brief 2012 *Scientific American* article "Snowflake Growth Successfully Modeled from Physical Laws," available online at www.scientificamerican.com/article/how-do-snowflakes-form.

Teaching with These Models

These models can be used to talk about ice and snow. But the approaches we use here in all the models of the chapter (of simplifying and using curve fits when the complexity is too high) can be used as a lesson as well. This aligns with the U.S. Next Generation Science Standards (NGSS) Engineering Technology and Application of Science (ETS2) Core Disciplinary Ideas about learning to break down a problem into solvable parts (www.nextgenscience.org/dci-arrangement/hs-ps2-motion-and-stability-forces-and-interactions). For example, we simplified the cone frustrum iceberg model significantly by fixing the ratio between the top and the bottom of the frustrum. Although this did not allow us to do every conceivable shape, it did allow the radius and height to be variable parameters.

Ice sheets collapsing into icebergs and how the freshwater in the icebergs is absorbed by the ocean may apply to earth science standards such as www.nextgenscience.org/pe/5-ess2-2-earths-systems, which looks at how freshwater and ocean water cycles interact.

Another concept we did not allude to directly in this chapter is the concept of finding volumes by displacement. Our calculation of how low any of the iceberg models should ride in the water could be used at several levels to talk about volumes of different solids, or Archimedes' Principle (https://en.wikipedia.org/wiki/Archimedes'_principle), which says that a body floating on water will displace a volume of water equal to its mass. These discussions can fit into the motion and stability forces and interactions standards at various grade levels.

Project Ideas

These models can be used to think about the role of melting ice in sea level change, or perhaps to motivate and help think about studying the ocean currents that carry icebergs for long distances. Projects about displacement, volume, and other basics might be more interesting in the context of water ice sailing the seas than it might be in the abstract. There are also new ecosystems being discovered under ice shelves, and the effects of huge sheets of ice being ripped from above these areas would be an interesting project to explore as well. The Larsen ice sheet disintegrations resulted in some discoveries along these lines.

Because the models in this chapter do have significant simplifications of the physics they represent, good student projects (at a variety of levels) could look at improving and expanding the models, or perhaps creating simulation or experimental data that then could inform these models. For example, given how our simple snowflake accretion model works, could you add a parameter or a second level of detail that could give more physical and more interesting results? What might be good next steps from this model? In the more experimental sphere, one could create a version of the snowflake microscope suggested at the end of Libbrecht's *Field Guide to Snowflakes* to take empirical data.

Summary

In this chapter we create models of icebergs and snowflakes. We also explore how icebergs calve from glaciers and then ride the seas 90% submerged as they erode and melt away. We discuss issues that arise when we want to model processes (like snowflake creation) that are too complex to model in detail with the tools available to us, and how to make reasonable engineering approximations. We also use Archimedes' Principle to think about how substances with different densities will displace water proportionate to their mass, and not their volume.

CHAPTER 4

■ ■ ■

Doppler and Mach

We have all had the experience of trying to figure out whether police and fire sirens are headed toward us or away. A siren coming closer will seem have a higher pitch than one going away.

The change in pitch is called the ***Doppler effect,*** and the actual change in frequency is called the ***Doppler shift***. It is named for Austrian mathematician and physicist Christian Doppler (1803–1853), who is credited for proposing it. It turns out that the Doppler effect applies to light waves as well as sound. Light from a source that is moving toward you has its frequency shifted higher, and light from something moving away shifts lower. One of the more exotic uses of this phenomenon is to track the movement of distant galaxies that are moving away from us.

Another Austrian who built on Doppler's work was Ernst Mach (1838–1916), a physicist and philosopher. His early work was focused on the Doppler effect in both optics and acoustics, not to mention philosophy (`https://plato.stanford.edu/entries/ernst-mach`). He is credited with taking the first photographs of bullets in flight and managing to capture an image of a ***shock wave***—a jump in pressure—that builds up ahead of something moving faster than the speed of sound. The way that shock wave builds up is closely related to the Doppler effect. We explore both of these phenomena in this chapter.

Doppler Effect

Imagine that a police car is driving away from you, siren blaring, pursuing a bad guy at 77 miles an hour. The speed of sound in air at sea level is about 340 meters per second, or 767 miles an hour. Thus the police car is driving away from you at about 10% of the speed of sound.

Now think about the sound waves from the siren spreading out as it moves. Because the car is moving at 10% of the speed of those waves, you can imagine the waves starting to pile up in front of the car because the siren keeps wailing while the car catches up to the sound it made before. Behind the car, on the other hand, the waves the siren has made are stretched out. The ***pitch*** of a sound is higher when the sound waves are closer together, and lower when they are more spread out.

© Joan Horvath and Rich Cameron 2017
J. Horvath and R. Cameron, *3D Printed Science Projects Volume 2*,
DOI 10.1007/978-1-4842-2695-7_4

Figure 4-1 shows a model of the waves generated by something putting out sound at a particular pitch while moving at 30% the speed of sound. Figure 4-2 shows a snapshot of the waves from a source at 80% the speed of sound. We have not included a model for the 10% speed of sound example because of the resolution of our model—it is pretty hard to see the effects of changes that small.

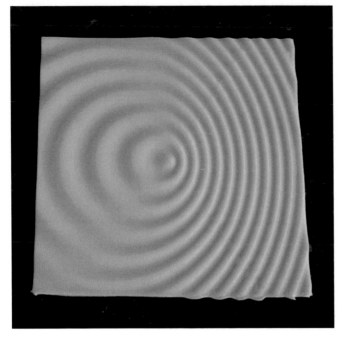

Figure 4-1. *Waves from a source moving to the right at 30% of the speed of sound*

Frequency Shift

The shifted frequency an observer hears from something moving ***toward*** them at a velocity ***v*** is determined by the equation

$$Shifted\ frequency = (1 + v / a) * (frequency\ at\ rest)$$

where ***a*** is the speed of sound. If the source of the sound is moving ***away***, the frequency changes like this:

$$Shifted\ frequency = (1 - v / a) * (frequency\ at\ rest)$$

Figure 4-2. *Waves from a source moving to the right at 80% of the speed of sound*

Think about the waves bunching up and getting closer together as the source moves toward you. The frequency ***rises*** as the distance between subsequent waves gets ***smaller***.

The ratio of a moving object's velocity to the speed of sound (the v / a term in the shifted frequency equation) is called the ***Mach number***, commonly denoted by ***M***. It is named in honor of Mach, but was not defined by him.

The speed of sound depends on the temperature of the air (or other gas) that is carrying the sound waves, and ambient density and pressure, all of which are interrelated. Warmer air will transmit the small physical disturbance of a sound wave from molecule to molecule faster. The molecules in hot, dense air are flying around faster and will more efficiently propagate a sound wave. For example, in the cold, thin air up where commercial airliners fly, at 10 kilometers (32,800 feet) above mean sea level, the speed of sound slows to 667 miles per hour from the 767 at sea level—a 13% decrease.

The Model

This model is based on the wave model in our earlier book ***3D Printed Science Projects*** (Apress, 2016; Chapter 2, "Light and Other Waves"). That model ultimately needs to get a set of points to plot out a 3D surface. In this case, because the source is moving, we need to work backwards from a point in ***x*** and ***y*** and figure out what wave would be passing over that point at a particular time.

We think about this by imagining that we are taking a snapshot at one particular time of all the waves that have been generated by our moving point source since it came into our field of view. Imagine that as the point source was flying along it puffed out a smoke ring on a regular basis. The oldest smoke rings would be the biggest, and the new ones the smallest. Instead of single smoke rings, though, we imagine our source is putting out a cosine wave at a particular frequency.

The waves from the moving source are traveling at the speed of sound. So we know that a wave that arrives at a particular point was generated by a source that was at the center of that circle at a time in the past. We can calculate that time by dividing the radius of the circle by the speed of sound. Figure 4-3 shows this situation, and we will work through the math to show you how we got our equations. We want to find **A**, the radius from where the wave (now at point (**x**,**y**)) started back when the disturbance was at **P1**. We show the point where the source is now as (0,0).

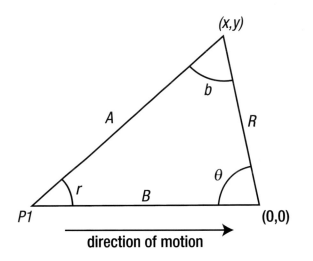

Figure 4-3. *Geometry to figure out which wave contributes to the amplitude at a particular point (x,y) at a particular snapshot in time*

We think of the object flying from **P1** to the current origin of its coordinate system in space, (0,0). We want to find the distance **A** in Figure 4-3 that is the distance of the posiition of the source when the wave was generated to the point (**x**,**y**).

We know the following to start with (based on the diagram in Figure 4-3):

- Our object creating the disturbance went from **P1** to (0,0) moving at Mach number **M**.

- The radius from the current position to the point (**x**,**y**)—we call this **R**.

- The angle theta, which is the angle with tangent **y** / **x**.

- That the angles in a triangle sum to 180 degrees.

- That **B** / **A** equals the Mach number **M** since the object moved **M** times the speed of sound times the time while the disturbance (moving at the speed of sound) moved from **P1** to (**x**,**y**).

To work out the math, we will use the law of sines, which says that for all the angles in a triangle, the ratios of the sine of all their angles to their opposite sides is equal. In this case, that would be:

$$sin(theta) / A = sin(b) / B = sin(r) / R$$

Since we know that $B/A = M$, use the relationships between the first two sides to get:

$$sin(theta) / A = sin(b) / MA \text{ (substituting } MA \text{ for } B)$$

Therefore, $b = asin(M * sin(theta))$
Next we need to get the third angle, r. Since the angles in a triangle add up to 180 degrees,

$$180 = theta + asin(M * sin(theta)) + r$$

or

$$r = 180 - theta - asin(M * sin(theta))$$

Going back to the original law of sines, we know that the angles *theta* and *r* are related like this:

$$sin(theta) / A = sin(r) / R$$

or

$$A = sin (theta) * R / sin (r)$$

Finally, to get A (which is what we wanted all along) we plug in the values we have found to get:

$$A = sin (theta) * R /$$

$$sin (180 - theta - asin(M * sin(theta)))$$

This is a peak of the cosine wave that was generated at *P1* in the past. The speed of the disturbance is Mach number times speed of sound. We are creating this whole snapshot at one (arbitrary) time, and so you can see that the actual values of time drop out in the algebra we just worked out.

Finally, we use that value of **amplitude * cos(A*frequency)** as the height of our wave at position (*x,y*) at our arbitrary time. Whew!

■ **Caution**   This model only applies below Mach 1. Beyond that, the source will outrun the waves, and the part of a new wave that is emitted behind the source will interfere (constructively and destructively) with the part of an old wave that was emitted forward. This form of the equation does not include that interference. It will have other problems, including one that results in what is called a *non-manifold* model for Mach numbers greater than or equal to 1. These models can cause problems for 3D printer software.

Listing 4-1. The Doppler Model

```
// File doppler.scad
// An OpenSCAD model of a snapshot of the waves
// around a moving object

// The model is based on the waves models in
// Volume 1 of 3D Printed Science Projects
// Rich "Whosawhatsis" Cameron, December 2016
// Units: lengths in mm, angles in degrees
// per OpenSCAD conventions
// This program creates a res*xmax mm by res*ymax rectangle
// As shown here will be 100 mm square.

// Model only valid for subsonic objects(mach < 1)

mach = .5; // mach number – must be less than 1.0
frequency = 20; // frequency - increase to show more waves
// setting frequency to high for the mach number will
// result in sampling artifacts
amplitude = .5; // Height of wave peaks on either side of the base plane, mm
thick = 2; // thickness of the slab, mm
xmax = 199; // max dimension in x (before scaling by res)
ymax = 199; //max dimension in x (before scaling by res)
res = .5; // scaling factor

// This function calculates a cosine wave with doppler shift:
function f(x, y) = amplitude * cos(r(x, y) / sin(theta(x, y)
+asin(sin(theta(x, y)) * mach)) * sin(theta(x, y)) * frequency);

// These two functions convert x/y values to polar coordinates:
function r(x, y, center = [xmax/2, ymax/2]) = sqrt(pow(center[0] - x, 2)
+pow(center[1] - y, 2));
function theta(x, y, center = [xmax/2, ymax/2]) = atan2((center[1] - y),
(center[0] - x));

// The rest of the model is the same as the
// wave model in Volume 1.
// It creates and interpolates a surface z = f(x,y)
// 3D printer conventions are that z is vertical –
// The model is rotated at the end
// so that the (x, y) surface is vertical, not horizontal
// This gives better print quality and allows for a wave
// surface on both sides of a print
// without support

toppoints = (xmax + 1) * (ymax + 1);
```

```
center = [xmax/2, ymax / 2];

points = concat(
    // top face
    [for(y = [0:ymax], x = [0:xmax]) [x, y, f(x, y)]],
    (thick ? //bottom face
        [for(y = [0:ymax], x = [0:xmax]) [x, y, f(x, y) - thick]]
    :
        [for(y = [0:ymax], x = [0:xmax]) [x, y, 0]]
    )
);

zbounds = [
    min([for(i = points) i[2]]),
    max([for(i = points) i[2]])
];

function quad(a, b, c, d, r = false) = r ?
    [[a, b, c], [c, d, a]]:
    [[c, b, a], [a, d, c]]; //create triangles from quad

faces = concat(
    //build top and bottom
    [for(
        bottom = [0, toppoints],
        i = [for(x = [0:xmax - 1],
        y = [0:ymax - 1]
    )
        quad(
            x + (xmax + 1) * (y + 1) + bottom,
            x + (xmax + 1) * y + bottom,
            x + 1 + (xmax + 1) * y + bottom,
            x + 1 + (xmax + 1) * (y + 1) + bottom,
            bottom
        )], v = i) v],
    //build left and right
    [for(i = [for(x = [0, xmax], y = [0:ymax - 1])
        quad(
            x + (xmax + 1) * y + toppoints,
            x + (xmax + 1) * y,
            x + (xmax + 1) * (y + 1),
            x + (xmax + 1) * (y + 1) + toppoints,
            x
        )], v = i) v],
    //build front and back
    [for(i = [for(x = [0:xmax - 1], y = [0, ymax])
        quad(
            x + (xmax + 1) * y + toppoints,
            x + 1 + (xmax + 1) * y + toppoints,
```

```
            x+1+(xmax+1) * y,
            x+(xmax+1) * y,
            y
      )], v=i) v]
);

// prevent an incorrect model from being generated
if(1>mach && mach>-1) {
   // Scale and rotate the print
   rotate([90, 0, 0]) scale([res, res, 1]) {
      polyhedron(points, faces);
   }
} else echo("mach number must be less than 1");
// end model
```

Printing and Changing the Model

As you saw in Figure 4-2, this model prints vertically—otherwise you would need to pick a lot of support off the model, and the waves would not print as cleanly. Because the model is very thin, we recommend against scaling it in your slicing software. Instead, change anything you want to in OpenSCAD. You can scale the model by changing the variable res, which multiplies the default size of 200 mm on a side (*res*=0.5 gives you 100 mm square pieces).

You can change the variable frequency to change the frequency of the wave the moving object is creating. The variable mach is the Mach number, which should be less than 1 for this model.

FOURIER TRANSFORMS

The problem of wanting to figure out what waves created a particular snapshot in time of a wave field (or the waves passing through a particular point) is not a new one. We generated a one-off geometrical answer for our problem here, but the general way of solving such problems is to use a technique called Fourier Transforms (https://en.wikipedia.org/wiki/Fourier_transform).

It requires some fairly solid knowledge of calculus to be able use these transforms. In a nutshell, though, you can either start out in "frequency space" with some known frequency distributions and use these techniques to see what the resulting patterns in space or time are, or you can go the other way around (as we did here) and deduce what waves contributed to a pattern at a particular position or time. Because they are very handy for many types of problems in signal processing and other fields, many different software packages exist to do "Digital Fourier Transforms" or "Fast Fourier Transforms." Search online on either term to find both open source and commercial software packages.

Mach Cone

Scientists associate Ernst Mach with several fundamental ideas, including **Mach's principle**, which laid out some ideas about how to think about motion that you can see relative to motions of far away objects, like the stars. Einstein depended on those ideas for his theory of general relativity later on. The biography *Einstein: A Hundred Years of Relativity* by Andrew Robinson (Princeton University Press: 2015) has some wonderful stories about how the young Einstein spent a lot of time studying Mach's work, and about how the two even met at one point.

More directly applicable to our discussion here is that Mach became interested in Doppler's work (a fellow Austrian) and started studying the implications of it. He became interested in the cases when something was moving faster than the speed of sound. He and a colleague pulled off the impressive feat (particularly for 1887) of photographing the waves generated by a bullet moving faster than the speed of sound.

He observed that the bullet creates a conical **shock wave** that moves with the bullet. In our era of supersonic aircraft, we call these shock waves **sonic booms** when they cross our path on the ground, and they are the extreme example of the bunching up of waves we saw in the previous section. Here, the object is moving so fast that it is catching up to and passing through the disturbances it is generating.

Shock Waves

Imagine that a plane is flying supersonically and making noise. The noise it made a second ago will be spreading out in a sphere, but the plane will have punched through that outer spreading sphere and moved on before the sphere gets there. This creates a shock wave angled away from the nose of plane at the **Mach angle**, which is an angle with a sine that is the reciprocal of the Mach number. At Mach 3, this is **asin(1 / 3)**, or about 19 degrees. The Mach cone's front will be twice the Mach angle, which you can verify from our models.

The Model

Our 3D printed model is shown in Figure 4-4 for a subsonic (Mach 0.5), transonic (Mach 1), and supersonic (Mach 3) case in which the vehicle is flying to the right of the picture at a 30-degree angle from the vertical.

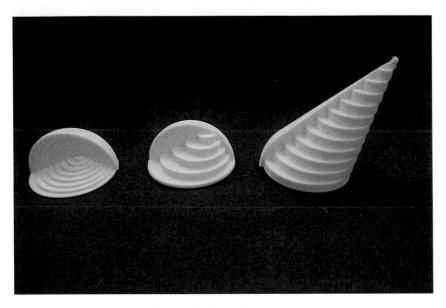

Figure 4-4. *Mach cone models for Mach 0.5, 1, and 3*

■ **Note** ***Transonic*** is the term for situations right around Mach 1, when we are transitioning from ***subsonic*** (below Mach 1) to ***supersonic*** (above it).

The model (Listing 4-2) is created by first making two spheres: one centered at the first modeled time with a radius that is the distance sound travels between that first modeled time and the current time, and a second sphere that is centered where the disturbance was just before its current position. OpenSCAD's hull() function is used to create a surface that contains these spheres and all the intermediate ones. This creates a smooth surface away from the stair steps that shows what the outer boundary of the sound traveling away would look like. The stair steps are cuts through the diameter of spheres at regular intervals along the direction of travel.

■ **Note** For Mach 1 and below, the traveling source has not outrun the oldest propagating sound wave, and so the outside is a sphere.

Figure 4-5 shows a different view of this envelope of the edge of the propagating waves for a supersonic point source moving to the right of the picture. We have shown both the 2D propagation of the edge of the disturbance from the moving point source (the circles) and the surface that defines the edge of all the disturbances if we made the steps between circles smaller and smaller.

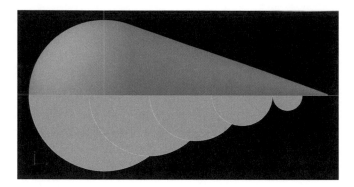

Figure 4-5. *2D projection of the Mach cone*

■ **Caution**   The bottom (largest) circle of the models should not be thought of as the ground cutting through a shock wave of something flying above it. The largest circle is just the radius of the disturbance from where we started keeping track of it.

Listing 4-2. The Mach Cone Model

```
// File machCone.scad
// An OpenSCAD model of a snapshot
// of the propagating disturbance
// From a point source moving at mach number, "mach"

// The model prints a disk that is a cross-section of
// the sphere representing a propagating disturbance
// from the traveling point source
// and a surface that is the envelope of
// the boundary of these propagating spheres
// Assumes point source at constant velocity

// Rich "Whosawhatsis" Cameron, December 2016
// Units: lengths in mm, angles in degrees,
// per OpenSCAD conventions

mach=0.5; // mach number

size=50; // diameter of the oldest propagation circle, in mm
a=30; // angle from the vertical at which
// the point source is traveling
step=3; // size of the circular cross-section steps
```

```
$fs = 2; // decrease this for smoother curves.
// This will slow down rendering.
$fa = 2;

// First section creates the outer boundary created by
// smoothing spheres of propagating
// disturbance as the point source moves
difference() {
    intersection() {
        hull() for(i = [1, size / 2]) {
            translate([sin(a), 0, cos(a)] * (size / 2 - i) * mach)
                sphere(r = i);
        }
        translate([-size, 0, 0]) cube(size * 10);
    }
    if(mach < = 1) for(i = [5:step:size / 2]) {
        translate([sin(a), 0, cos(a)] * (size / 2 - i) * mach) {
            rotate([90, 0, 0]) {
                linear_extrude(2, center = true) difference() {
                    circle(i);
                    circle(i - .2);
                }
            }
        }
    }
} // end difference

// Next create the stair steps representing the diameter of
// propagation circles
intersection() {
    for(i = [0:step:size / 2+step]) {
        translate([sin(a), 0, cos(a)] * (size / 2 - i) * mach) {
            cylinder(
                r = i,
                h = step * mach * cos(a)+.01,
                center = true
            );
        }
    }
    translate([-size, -size * 10, 0]) cube(size * 10);
}

// end model
```

Printing and Changing the Model

As with the Doppler model, we suggest you do not scale this model down with your printer's scaling; change anything you want to in the model itself by changing the variable size, which is the diameter of the largest (bottom) circle in mm. The variable mach is the Mach number. Scaling it up should work, although you may see some of the facets of the approximations making up the model if you scale it too much outside of OpenSCAD.

THINKING ABOUT THESE MODELS: LEARNING LIKE A MAKER

The most difficult thing about these models was getting the geometry right, particularly for the Doppler effect model. Although the basic idea is simple, figuring out the height of the model in a snapshot in time was tricky (as you can see in the section describing the logic). We felt better when we realized that we had more or less reinvented Fourier transforms.

The very hardest part of all, though, was making sure the models were right. Rich reads geometry problems like most people read romance novels, considering them lightweight and obvious. Joan is more algebraically inclined, and we took about ten times as long validating the Doppler model as initially conceiving it. The Mach cone model was developed first and provided the mental model for the Doppler one.

Where to Learn More

The topics in this chapter are typically covered at the undergraduate college level, although they are certainly good fodder for more advanced K-12 physics students and their science fair projects. As such, we relied heavily on Joan's college textbooks for key numbers and equations.

For standard atmosphere values of the speed of sound and background on Mach numbers, we relied on the textbook *Foundations of Aerodynamics, 3rd edition* (Wiley, 1976) by Kuethe and Chow. It looks like a 5th edition was published in 1997. For more details on the physics of the Doppler effect, we used Morse and Ingard's *Theoretical Acoustics* (McGraw-Hill, 1968).

We did not explictly go into light waves here, but you can read about the Doppler shift applied to light if you look up "redshift" (https://en.wikipedia.org/wiki/Redshift) or "expansion of the universe." The universe *is* expanding, and so all galaxies are flying away from each other in a way that makes light from them seem shifted toward the red end of the spectrum (that is, waves from them get stretched farther apart, sort of like the descending pitch when a sound is moving away). However, light is not as straightforward to model as sound because of relativistic effects—how a situation "looks" for moving light sources depends on where and when you are observing.

Teaching with These Models

As we noted in the last section, these topics are most commonly covered in undergraduate or graduate physics courses. However, these models might be interesting to include as talking points when teaching the concept of waves in general, for instance under the Next Generation Science Standards (NGSS) HS-PS4-1, "Use mathematical representations to support a claim regarding relationships among the frequency, wavelength, and speed of waves traveling in various media" (www.nextgenscience.org/pe/hs-ps4-1-waves-and-their-applications-technologies-information-transfer). More general discussions of sound waves and perhaps of other periodic functions could also be supported using these models as visualizations of interesting test cases.

Project Ideas

These models are visualizations (models meant to give you intuition). However, you can change the Mach number and frequency. In the case of the Doppler plots, raising the frequency in essence raises the resolution of the plot, to a point. If you raise it too far, you will start to create artifacts, since the models are (by default) just 199 points across in each dimension. If you lower it too much, you may be zoomed in too far to see more than a wave or two, and you will not see the Doppler effect then either. The same is true for the step size in the Mach cone models.

For the same reason, be careful about scaling these models down in your printer software. They may get too thin to print vertically, or develop artifacts in the prints of the waves.

With all that said, you might find it interesting to print each of the models in this chapter for a few Mach numbers and several frequencies to build your intuition about how these effects look in 2D snapshots (the first model) and in 3D. Remember, though, that the Doppler model (Listing 4-1) must be used only below Mach 1.

You also might look at what the equivalent models would look like for light. We did not embark on them because of the complications that ensue when you think about relativisitic effects.

Summary

This chapter discusses sound waves created by moving objects. The first model visualizes the Doppler-shifted waves created by something moving through air or another medium at speeds below the speed of sound. The second model is a little more general. It looks at 3D snapshots of the outer boundary of disturbances caused by objects moving either above or below the speed of sound. Above the speed of sound, these disturbances create a Mach cone around themselves, which separates where the disturbance from the moving object has propagated from where it has not. We conclude with some ideas about how to use these models to build intuition.

CHAPTER 5

■ ■ ■

Moment of Inertia

Designing spinning or rotating machines can be complex and generally requires a bit of calculus. However, we can look at some simplified cases and design a few pieces that can help you analyze the motion of spinning—or in the case of this chapter, rolling—objects. Here we will develop a simple, basic rolling cylinder with internal structures that you can adapt to look into the physics of this deceptively simple-appearing motion.

Rolling Motion

If a wheel is perched at the top of a hill, before it starts moving it has **potential energy**, and that energy has the potential to be turned into motion. Once it starts **rolling** downhill (not slipping or sliding), the wheel is using energy to do two things: rotate about its center of mass and move (a physicist would say **translate**) down the slope. The rotational part depends on how the mass inside the wheel is distributed, and that mass distribution is what we will vary in our experiments in this chapter. If we decide that for now we will not worry about friction and other things that dissipate energy, we can write the **conservation of energy** like this:

Potential energy = Translational energy + Rotational energy

Potential energy for a wheel at the top of a hill is equal to the mass of the wheel times the height above some reference baseline (say, the bottom of the hill) times the acceleration caused by gravity, usually referred to as **g**. The value of **g** on Earth is about 980 cm/s². If the height of the slope is **h** and the total mass of the wheel is **M**, then the potential energy is equal to $M * g * h$.

The translational energy is how fast the wheel is moving down the slope. It is proportional to the mass times the square of its velocity down the slope. If we call that velocity v, the translational energy is $(1/2) * M * v^2$.

The rotational energy is a little trickier. How much does the wheel turn in some set amount of time? The wheel is speeding up as it goes down the slope, because gravity is accelerating it. We can think about the point of contact where the wheel touches the ground as moving at angular velocity v / R. The total rotational energy is equal to $(1/2) * I * v^2 / R^2$, where R is the radius of the wheel and **I** is the **moment of rotational inertia**, typically just called the moment of inertia.

© Joan Horvath and Rich Cameron 2017
J. Horvath and R. Cameron, *3D Printed Science Projects Volume 2*,
DOI 10.1007/978-1-4842-2695-7_5

■ **Note**   Angular velocity has units of ***radians per second*** divided by time and is the inverse of the time it takes for the wheel to rotate one radian. There are 2π radians in one turn of the wheel, or 360 degrees equals 2π radians. If you imagine a piece of string the length of the radius of a circle and you take that string and lay it along that circle, the angle inside that arc is one radian.

Moment of Inertia

The moment of inertia has units of mass times the square of distance and is a measure of how hard it is to get something to start (or stop) rolling. In that way, it acts sort of like a mass in that if the energy input is equal, if the moment of rotational inertia goes up, the wheel will turn more slowly.

■ **Tip**   You can think about it like this: mass measures how much something resists acceleration in a straight line, and moment of inertia measures resistance to angular acceleration.

The moment of inertia is equal to the sum of all the masses that make up an object times the square of their distance from the center of mass. So, the more mass is moved out away from the center of mass, the more energy it takes to turn the wheel once because the radius of the mass is getting bigger.

The model for the chapter, shown in Figure 5-1, looks like a hockey puck with holes punched in it. We call it the ***weighted wheel***. The one we used in this chapter, printed in PLA with 10% infill, has a mass without any pennies in it of 46 grams. There are penny-sized holes into which we can place coins to add mass at different radii from the center.

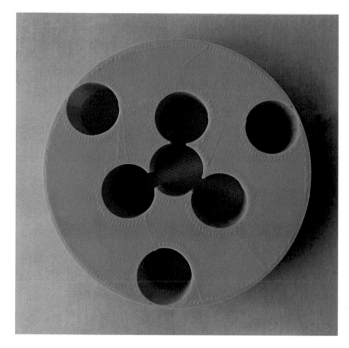

Figure 5-1. *The weighted wheel model*

■ **Note**   We use centimeters and grams or, more generally, the cgs (centimeter-gram-second) unit system in this chapter. First, the natural units of what we are measuring are centimeters and grams, because we are working at the scale of everyday objects. Secondly, because of that, school physics labs (where we expect many of our readers reside) often work in these units for the same reason. However, 3D printers typically measure in millimeters, so you will need to convert centimeters to millimeters if you want to change anything in the model (1 cm = 10 mm).

Use a bit of tape (blue tape of the type used on 3D printer platforms works nicely—see Figure 5-2) to hold pennies in place by wrapping a set of pennies in blue tape. We found that the pennies fell out if we just put blue tape over the holes, and if they rattled a bit it affected the results. We used slugs of 13 pennies per hole for the experiments in this chapter.

Figure 5-2. *The weighted wheel model with pennies in the "outer ring" held with blue tape*

Predicted Moments of Inertia for This Model

For the model in Figures 5-1 and 5-2, we will figure out the moment of rotational inertia as follows:

> ***Moment of rotational inertia = Rotational inertia of the wheel + Sum of the rotational inertias of the pennies***

Wikipedia (`https://en.wikipedia.org/wiki/Moment_of_inertia`) and other physics references tell us that the moment of inertia of a solid cylinder is *(1/2) * M * R²*. Our model is not a solid cylinder—it is a 3D print with an outer shell, some holes in it, and 10% infill—but for getting general trends, it should be close enough. In this case, the radius **R** is 50 mm, or 5 cm. With a mass of 46 grams, we get the moment of inertia of the empty wheel without coins as 575 g-cm².

Simplest Approximation: Pennies as Point Masses

For a first cut at figuring out the center of mass, we will treat the pennies as point masses at their centers. A ***point mass*** contributes its mass times the square of its radius from the center of mass of the overall object to the moment of rotational inertia. Later we give suggestions for doing this more accurately, but for now we want to give a rough idea about how to get started.

We used 39 pennies for our experiments, 13 in each of the sets of 3 holes. We measured the mass as 100 grams total. As noted in Chapter 1, some pennies are 3 g and some are 2.5, depending on when they were minted (they were heavier before 1982). We felt that just weighing them was a simple measurement and would allow for wear. All the holes are 20 mm in diameter, just a bit bigger than the 19.5 mm diameter of a penny.

The centers of the outer penny holders are 0.1 cm plus 10 cm in from the outside of the wheel's 5 cm radius; that works out to 5 - 0.1 - 1 = 3.9 cm. The additional rotational moment of inertia for pennies in the outer ring is thus 100 g * (3.9 cm)^2, or 1521 g-cm^2. The overall moment of inertia for the empty wheel plus pennies in the outer circle of holes is 575 + 1521 = 2096 g-cm^2.

The center of the inner ring of three pennies are halfway between the outer penny holders and the hole at the center of the wheel; that is, 1.95 cm. So, the additional rotational moment of inertia added by pennies in the inner ring is 100 g * (1.95 cm)^2, or 380 g-cm^2, making the overall moment of inertia for the empty wheel plus pennies on the inner circle of holes 575 + 380 = 955 g-cm^2.

Finally, we placed 13 pennies in the central hole; we used 100 / 3 grams as the mass for this. If we are treating the pennies as a point mass at the center, the moment of inertia does not change and is the same as the empty wheel, or 575 g-cm^2. The mass, though, is different. Table 5-1 sums up these results.

Table 5-1. *Moment of Inertia for Three Cases*

Case	Mass (g)	Moment of Inertia (g-cm^2)	Moment/mass (cm^2)
No pennies	46	575	12.5
Pennies inner ring	146	955	6.54
Pennies outer ring	146	2096	14.3
Pennies concentric	80	575	7.19

Improving the Estimate: Parallel Axis Theorem

The moment of inertia can be calculated about any axis that is fixed with respect to the body itself. So far we have talked about the case of a circular object rotating around its center, but the more general case requires a few more tools.

The point-mass approximation will give a somewhat low value for moment of inertia. The next best approximation would be to treat each stack of pennies as a ***cylinder*** of mass 33 grams and radius 0.975 cm. Then we would use the ***parallel axis theorem*** which says that the moment of inertia of a distinct part of a bigger object (like our pennies in the cylinder) is equal to its moment of inertia about its own center, added to its mass times the square of the distance from its center of mass to the overall object's center of mass. In the case here, we would compute this for the inner ring pennies as follows: moment of inertia of a stack of pennies (a cylinder) about its center is equal to *(1 / 2)* * *M* * *R*^{2}, where ***M*** is the mass of our average stack of pennies or 33 grams, and ***R*** is 0.975 cm. Multiplying this out, we get 15.7 g-cm^2.

Now to get the moment of inertia of these pennies about the overall body's center of mass, we use the distance between the two centers of mass times the mass of the stack of pennies to see what the moment of inertia is about the center of the wheel. This distance, as we established earlier, is 3.9 cm.

So, this term adds 33 grams times 3.9 cm squared, or 502 g-cm^2 for a total of 15.7 + 502 = 518 g-cm^2 per stack. For the three outer pennies plus the wheel itself, we get 3 * 518 + 575 (empty moment of inertia) or a total of 2128 g-cm^2, versus the 2096 we got with the point-mass assumption.

Predicting Velocity of the Rolling Wheel

Once we have these numbers, we can predict how fast the wheel should roll downhill. First, we need to compute a formula for the velocity the wheel will have after it rolls down the slope of our experiment, when it will have converted all its potential energy (at the top of the slope) to kinetic and rotational energy. As mentioned in the last section, we know:

Potential energy = Translational energy + Rotational energy

Combining the formulas for each term from the last section gives us:

$$M * g * h = (1 / 2) * M * v^2 + (1 / 2) * I * v^2 / R^2$$

Which we can clean up a bit to this:

$$2 * g * h = v^2 * (1 + I / (M * R^2))$$

Or solving for velocity,

$$v^2 = 2 * g * h / (1 + I / (M * R^2))$$

where **g** = 980 cm/s^2, **R** = 5 cm, **h** = **distance** * **sin(incline angle)**, and **I** = moment of inertia. If we want to get the ratio of the velocities for our current weighted wheel cases, we get the following equation, after dividing out some of the things that we can hold constant from one test to another (like the geometry of the slope, the distance travelled, and so on, assuming here the radius R of the overall body is the same):

$$v_1 / v_2 = sqrt ((1 + I_2 / (M_2 * R^2)) / (1 + I_1 / (M_1 * R^2)))$$

The results of plugging in some pairs of values for comparisons are shown in Table 5-2. The moments of inertia vary, but the masses do too. Because this is a dynamic system, the results can be a little surprising. The higher the moment of inertia, the slower the wheel will accelerate, and longer it will take to reach the bottom of the slope. However, the higher moment of inertia in some cases was offset by differences in mass.

Table 5-2. *Velocity Ratios Predicted for Some Combinations*

Case	Predicted velocity ratio
No pennies: 39 pennies inner ring	1 : 1.09
No pennies: 39 pennies outer ring	1 : 0.98
39 pennies inner ring : 39 outer ring	1.12 : 1

Results

We tried rolling the wheel on a smooth table with one end raised up a bit, and also outdoors on some sloping concrete. We took our weighted wheel out, rolled it in the configurations in Table 5-1, and measured the distance rolled and the time.

■ **Tip** To get the starting height for our outdoor trial, we used a cell phone bubble-level app (iHandy Level on an iPhone, Multi Clinometer on an Android phone) to measure the angle of the incline. That plus how far the wheel rolled gives us the height difference between the start and end of the test run. Distance rolled times the sine of the slope of the inclined table will give the height difference between the start and stop times.

Rolling it outdoors encountered a variety of problems. The concrete was not very smooth, and had decorative inlaid bricks. The empty wheel stopped very soon after starting and in some cases even rolled backward (in the nominally uphill direction) a bit! However, qualitatively it was interesting to see how much faster the wheel rolled with the pennies on the inside versus the outside.

We would expect the velocity calculated by $v^2 = 2*g*h / (1 + I / (M * R^2))$ to be twice the average velocity over the whole time rolling down the table, because gravity is making it accelerate. We got the average velocity by just dividing the distance the wheel rolled by the time it took to travel it.

The first setup we used was a smooth table 150 cm long, raised 3.14 cm at one end. We let the wheel go on one end and recorded at least three times how long it took each configuration to cross the far end (Figure 5-3). A strategic pillow on a chair and another on the floor at the end is good for catching it so it does not break or dump pennies everywhere when it goes off the edge.

Figure 5-3. *The empty wheel heading downhill (to the upper right in the photo) to its pillows*

The second setup was outdoors on some gently sloping concrete. We tried to note when the wheel got to 12 feet (366 cm) centered where we were releasing it, trying to repeat the initial release angle as much as possible. We marked our starting spot with a bit of blue tape (Figure 5-4) and you can take advantage, as we did, of decorative markings as start or stop points. It is not a perfect solution because the slope will vary, but the wheels did not roll all that repeatably and other things we tried (see the "Learning Like a Maker" section of this chapter) had other issues. We found an average slope of 3 degrees on the concrete and used that to calculate a height difference of 19.1 cm in 366 cm.

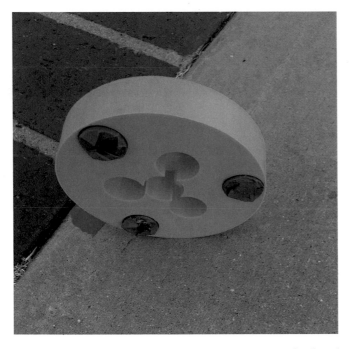

Figure 5-4. *Marking the start of a test run on concrete for the wheel with the pennies on the outer ring. Downhill is to the right.*

Table 5-3 summarizes these results. We predicted the velocity based on the moment of inertia calculated and the measured heights of the ramps, and then divided by 2 to compare it to the average velocity (just the distance over the time). The empty ring and pennies in center models were only tested indoors. The empty wheel was too easily perturbed by random bumps in the concrete to get any repeatability.

Table 5-3. *Measurements*

Case	½ Final v, Predicted	Average Velocity, Measured
Inner ring, outdoors	86	75
Outer ring, outdoors	77	66
Inner ring, indoors	35	33
Outer ring, indoors	32	30
13 pennies in center, indoors	35	29
Empty ring, indoors	32	28

As the physics predicts, higher moment of inertia wheels go more slowly. The measured ratio of the speeds of the wheel with pennies on the inner ring to the outer is 1.14 : 1 outdoors and 1.09 : 1 indoors, bracketing our theoretical ratio of 1.12 : 1 in Table 5-2. There is, of course, a spread in the results because of the many uncertainties, which we note in the following Caution.

■ **Caution**   Measuring the angle of a ramp is challenging, and if you choose to try an outdoor patio or playground you will find that slopes vary, even if to the eye they do not. We had many interactions with curious bugs. Concrete is also rough, and friction and breezes are a factor, and sometimes a teeny push was needed to get the wheel rolling. Of course, you need to do this someplace where you can set up safely and without interruption, such as a backyard patio or long sloping walkway. We tried outdoors since our runs on the tilted table were just 5 seconds or so, and timing with a stopwatch app on a phone for sub-second accuracy is possible but challenging. Finally, our assumptions for calculating the moment of inertia of this asymmetrical body (because of the solid bottom) are simplified. In this chapter's "Project Ideas" section we make some suggestions on how you might improve it. Nonetheless, the trends are correct, and we enjoyed building our intuition as we went.

The Model

The 3D-printable model for the wheel, shown in Listing 5-1, is very simple. It starts with a cylinder and subtracts other cylinders from it. The parameter coin is the diameter of the coins you want to use (plus a bit of margin—we used 20 mm for 19.5 mm diameter pennies, which left room for tape around them).

You can vary the diameter, d, to make a bigger or smaller wheel too. If you change the diameter, holes will remain near the edge, but the ring nearer the center will move outward to be halfway between the center hole and the outer ones. Obviously, you cannot make this a lot smaller than it is now. The radius ***R*** we use in previous sections is one-half the diameter d.

The model is pretty straightforward to print. This one is 20 mm high (2 cm), which accommodates 13 pennies. We tried making one with quarter-sized holes and making it thinner, but it was too unstable.

■ **Note**   Listing 5-1 uses millimeters (as is conventional in 3D printing), but our calculations elsewhere in this chapter are in centimeters to make the numbers a little easier to handle. Be careful to keep track of that if you change anything.

Listing 5-1. The Weighted Wheel

```
// A model of a weighted wheel
// To demonstrate conservation of angular momentum
// file weightedWheel.scad
// Rich Cameron, March 2017

d=100; // diameter of disk, in mm
h=20; //height of disk, in mm
t=1; // minimum wall thicknesses
coin=20; // diameter of coin in use, mm

$fs=.2;
$fa=2;

difference() {
    cylinder(r=d / 2, h=h);
    for(i=[0:6]) rotate(120 * i+60 * ceil(i / 3))
        translate([ceil(i / 3) * (d - coin - t * 2) / 4, 0, t])
            cylinder(r=coin / 2, h=h);
} // end model
```

3D printed "cylinders" are made up of small flat surfaces. If you want the wheel to be made up of smaller increments (and thus be rounder and smoother) change the $fs and $fa parameters. In OpenSCAD, the number of faces in the regular polygons used to approximate circles are specified using the special $fs, $fa, and $fn special variables. $fs specifies the minimum size of the facets in mm, with a default of 2 mm. $fa is the minimum angle between facets in degrees, defaulted to 12 degrees. Depending on the size of the object you are printing, one or the other will be important, as follows:

- For small, circular 3D printed objects, $fs will keep the number of facets high enough to make the circle look round. A small-enough value for $fs will prevent holes from ending up too much smaller than the specified diameter. This is because the radius of a regular polygon is measured from the center to the vertices, and the *apothem* (the distance from the center of the polygon to the center of a side) is smaller.

- For larger circular objects, a larger $fa value will prevent the number of facets from becoming unnecessarily high, which increases rendering time. $fa needs to be a number that divides evenly into 360 (if it is not, OpenSCAD will round to a number that is).

- $fn overrides both of the other special variables and allows the user to specify a specific number of facets. It is usually a bad idea to set $fn globally. Any of these variables can also be specified for each individual object, which provides an easy way to create a regular polygon of $fn sides.

Other Models

Fidget spinner toys are currently popular of late, and there are many on Thingiverse—Rich made one starting from a toy he found at www.thingiverse.com/thing:1802260. These use radial ball bearings (typically size 608, which are used in skateboards and are thus easy to find) to spin while you play with them (Figure 5-5). This design will even spin on a table (Figure 5-6). If you want to play with something of constant mass and the ability to spin about different arms, you may want to join the fidget spinner craze (though it is a fad that may already be over by the time you read this).

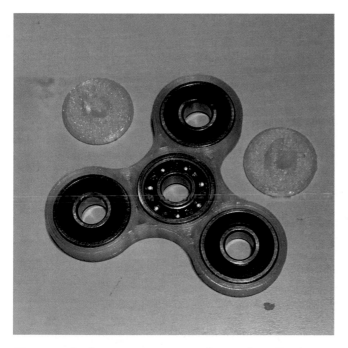

Figure 5-5. *Fidget spinner: 3D printed parts plus roller skate bearings*

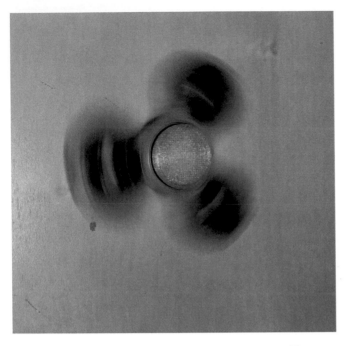

Figure 5-6. *Fidget spinner in motion, spinning on a table*

THINKING ABOUT THESE MODELS: LEARNING LIKE A MAKER

Our weighted wheel, like many we have created, seemed simple. We wanted to create something that would give some intuition on rotational inertia, which can be very counterintuitive. We thought about propellers and other things that spin on an axis, but it is challenging to get a 3D printed part that spins freely without also asking people to go out and buy bearings. There are 3D-printable bearings (see the first volume of our *3D Printed Science Projects* books) but anything more than printing a bearing on its own gets challenging.

After lengthy brainstorming, we hit on this model. The first one was designed for quarters, was thinner than this one, and fell over continually. We made this one thicker and at least it would stand up. We also considered making a skeletal model, a hoop with spokes, for instance, to reduce the mass and print time of the wheel, but determined that it would likely end up using more material than printing a "solid" wheel with minimal infill.

However, when we tried rolling the model on a table for the first time, we were surprised at how fast it went and how hard it was to use a stopwatch on a phone to sub-second accuracy. Initially we allowed the wheel to roll variable distances and measured time and distance, but that was too confusing, and it was likely the slopes were varying, too, in the outdoor case. The empty wheel just turned around and sometimes started rolling uphill if it hit a bump or a bug—we gave up and just took that data on the smooth table as best we could with our limited timing equipment.

We finally came up with a two-person timing process. One person would hold the wheel, the other would start a counter and start counting, and the wheel was released three seconds in. The person with the stopwatch would stand at the downhill side and record when the wheel went off the table or crossed the concrete markings. Then we subtracted three seconds from all data. Then we found out how uneven even a very smooth-looking swath of concrete can be (and how many small bugs go out for a stroll on a sunny California spring day).

This model (and the experiment design) can be adapted and improved in many ways, as we talk about in the "Projects" section. But even just rolling it down a table propped up on a couple of books at one end can give you some surprises.

Where to Learn More

Moment of inertia is typically covered in a freshman physics class that requires or is taught concurrently with a calculus class. We used Joan's college textbook, the 1977 edition of Resnick and Halliday's *Physics* (Wiley), the most recent version of which seems to be a fifth edition (Wiley, 2001). If you do not want to splash out for and cannot borrow an expensive text, Wikipedia's article on moment of inertia (https://en.wikipedia.org/wiki/Moment_of_inertia) is quite good, as are various related articles (particularly "Rotational Dynamics: Rolling Spheres/Cylinders") on http://physicslab.org. You might search on "rolling without slipping" to find the types of problems that this model might help you think about. Physics book chapters that discuss topics like this probably have something like *rotational dynamics* in their titles.

Teaching with These Models

In the United States, material relevant to this chapter is typically taught in a freshman college or AP physics course, where it can benefit from the application of calculus concepts. If you are teaching at the K-12 level, though, we can imagine that some of the experiments we describe in "Project Ideas" could build some intuition under the standards for Forces and Actions (www.nextgenscience.org/topic-arrangement/hsforces-and-interactions) even if you did not want to wade into calculating moment of inertia.

If you do have students that are comfortable with the algebra you might have them calculate moment of inertia for various objects they design and predict how fast they will roll, based on the equations in this chapter. You can also talk about experimental error and how much accuracy to expect.

We think it would also be fun to use this model as a starting point for a high school physics or undergrad challenge to have a contest to make the slowest, fastest or longest roll on a nice smooth sloping school pathway, or to most closely hit a particular average or final velocity. To do that you would have to take friction and other forces into account, too.

Projects

If you are trying to build your own intuition or come up with a project to teach others, you could start with the challenge just mentioned. To have that degree of precision, you would need to improve the accuracy of the moment of inertia calculation. Some options are to treat the pennies as cylinders and not point masses, as described in the earlier section that calculates the moment of inertia. You could consider changes to the geometry of the empty cylinder. The references listed under "Where to Learn More" have formulas for moments of inertia of other shapes such as hoops, spheres, and so on.

In addition to improving the calculations, you can improve how you measure time and the inclination of your slope. Using a longer, presumably outdoor slope means you do not have to be quite as good at measuring time, but it is unlikely that you have access to a perfectly sloped and smoothed ramp. You could consider ways to keep the wheel rolling straight without dissipating too much energy in friction.

You can explore ways of measuring the time more accurately. We like the *Mythbusters* TV show episode setup to measure the speed of a sneeze, which you could adapt if you have the ability to step through video frame by frame (`www.discovery.com/tv-shows/mythbusters/videos/slow-motion-sneezes/`). The model was designed to fit on a relatively small 3D printer. If you have a bigger printer, you could make a bigger wheel and compare predicted and measured moments of inertia, or try more complex arrangements of coins or other weights.

Summary

This chapter creates a 3D-printable model that allows exploration of the concept of moment of inertia of a rolling cylinder. First we define moment of inertia, as the resistance of a body to rolling motion, analogous the resistance to motion in a straight line caused by the body's mass. We review how to calculate moment of inertia starting with a simplistic approximation and moving on to slightly better ones. We do some simple experiments using the model and show ways to make both the calculation and the experiment better, at the cost of more complexity. Finally, we end with ways to improve the calculations, as well as projects that could use this chapter's model as a jumping-off point.

CHAPTER 6

■ ■ ■

Probability

We all toss around words like *likely* and *impossible*, but we rarely try to quantify what they mean. That job is left to experts in probability and statistics. Often our perception of how likely something is has very little to do with how likely it *really* is, which is good news for people who run state lotteries.

How likely something is can be expressed in terms of a *probability distribution*. For example, if you have a six-sided die and it is weighted fairly, you would expect it to be equally probable that the die would land on any side. This is called a *uniform distribution*. However, things get interesting when you see what happens when you roll several dice at once. Fans of role-playing games that involve throwing several dice (perhaps to see how much your fighter's greatsword damages the dragon) will enjoy getting some insight in this chapter's sidebar.

The values of many natural phenomena more or less follow a *normal* distribution, which means that the likelihood of, say, how tall a woman in the United States is follows a bell-shaped curve (Figure 6-1) of the values spread out symmetrically around an average value, called the *mean* (in this case, 64 inches, or 1.6 meters).

Figure 6-1. *Normal distribution model (with a base)*

In this chapter we create models of several different probability distributions, including some that visualize more than one random variable at a time. These *multivariate* distributions are hard to visualize on paper, making them great opportunities for 3D printing.

© Joan Horvath and Rich Cameron 2017
J. Horvath and R. Cameron, *3D Printed Science Projects Volume 2*,
DOI 10.1007/978-1-4842-2695-7_6

Normal Distribution

A graph of a normal distribution is a 2D thing that you can draw on a piece of paper. But what happens when you want to explore the probability distribution of two random variables that may or may not be related with each other? This is called a **multivariate** (or, in the case of two variables, **bivariate**) probability function. First we need to understand what a single-variable normal distribution looks like.

The Math

A normal distribution curve, as you saw in Figure 6-1, always has a shape sort of like a bell and thus is sometimes called a bell curve. The shape is always roughly similar, but whether it is a low, wide bell or a tall, skinny one and where it is centered are defined by two numbers. The first of those numbers is the **mean**, the average value of the variable we are studying (and also the most likely value, at the peak of the distribution). The mean determines the position of the center of the curve. Another number called the **standard deviation** (typically represented by σ, the Greek letter sigma) determines how much the distribution spreads out around the mean.

A very useful property of the normal distribution is that 68% of the values are within one σ either side of the mean, 95% are within 2σ, and 99.7% are within 3σ. The mean and standard deviation have the same units as each other. If we assume that the diameters of peaches picked on a farm could be represented by a bell curve, both the mean and standard deviations would be in inches or millimeters or however the farmer described his peaches.

We would know that if the mean diameter of the farmer's peaches is 2.5 inches with a standard deviation of 0.1 inch that 68% of the peaches would have diameters between 2.4 and 2.6 inches (plus and minus one sigma). The standard deviation gives us the height at the center of the distribution (at the mean) of $1 / (\sigma\sqrt{2\pi})$.

The edges of the curve (far from the center of the bell) are called the *tails*. They never quite reach zero, theoretically, but it is unlikely that any randomly selected value will fall there, just as it is unlikely that our farmer will discover a 4-inch-diameter peach.

■ **Note** We use both mathematical notation and pseudocode in this chapter. For the most part, in our equations we will not use * for **multiply** because it would get too unwieldy; math expressions like $2\sigma_x$ will become **2 * SDx** in the OpenSCAD model. We also use several different types of parentheses in our math equations for typographical clarity. These parentheses mean specific things in OpenSCAD and do not translate directly to it.

The equation for the bell-shaped probability curve for one variable, x, is:

$$P(x) = [1 / (\sqrt{2\pi\sigma^2}\,)]\, exp[-(x - mean\ of\ x)^2 / (2\sigma^2)]$$

Where *exp* is the *exponential* function, $exp(x) = e^x$, and *e* is *Euler's number*, roughly 2.71. If instead of just one normally-distributed variable, though, we have two, *x* and *y*, their *joint probability* function is the following:

$$P(x,y) = [1 / (2\pi \sigma_x \sigma_y \sqrt{1 - \rho^2})] * exp([-1/(2(1 - \rho^2))] * [X + Y + C]), \text{ where}$$

$$X = (x - \text{mean of } x)^2 / \sigma_x^2, \; Y = (y - \text{mean of } y)^2 / \sigma_y^2,$$

$$C = 2\rho \; (x - \text{mean of } x)(y - \text{mean of } y) / (\sigma_x \sigma_y), \text{ and}$$

σ_x, σ_y = standard deviations of the x and y variables.

The Greek letter ρ (rho) requires a bit of explanation. It is the correlation coefficient (as we use it here, technically, the Pearson correlation coefficient) between *x* and *y*. Here is how to interpret ρ:

- If $\rho = 0$, the two variables are not linearly correlated—they might be correlated in some other way, though.

- If $\rho = 1$, the variables are perfectly linearly correlated with each other, and if you graphed *x* versus *y* the points (x,y) would form a straight line.

- If $\rho = -1$, they are perfectly linearly anticorrelated (one goes up while the other goes down), and again you would get a straight line which sloped downward.

- For other values of ρ the points (x,y) would form a scatter plot, clustering more as the value of ρ got closer to 1 or –1.

We are going to explore a few cases to get some intuition. In what follows in this chapter we will just pick a value of ρ. If you started with (x,y) data, you would calculate ρ (along with the means and standard deviations) from your data. For more on this, see https://en.wikipedia.org/wiki/Pearson_correlation_coefficient, https://en.wikipedia.org/wiki/Multivariate_normal_distribution or search on "correlation coefficient" at the Khan Academy, www.khanacademy.org.

The Models

Now, let's see what it looks like if we create a 3D model of the **P(x,y)** normal distribution. Figure 6-1 is a side view of the case in which the means and standard deviations of the two distributions are the same. In Figure 6-2, the means are the same but one standard deviation is three times that of the other. That means that lines of equal probability (the same height) are circles in Figure 6-1 and ellipses in Figure 6-2. In both cases, $\rho - 0$. It is worth noting that the flat areas on Figure 6-2 are not zero probability, but just so low that they are below the resolution the print can show.

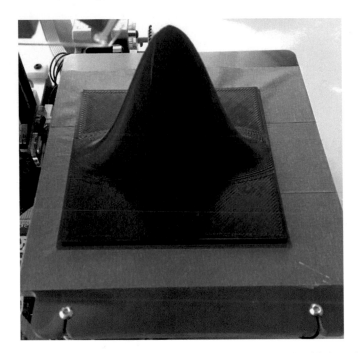

Figure 6-2. *Normal distribution: standard deviation in side-to-side direction is three times that in front-to-back direction.*

■ **Note** This model builds on the math surface plotting function in Chapter 1 of Volume 1 of our previous book *3D Printed Science Projects* (2016, Apress).

Listing 6-1. Two-Variable Normal Distribution Model

```
// Probability distribution function of two variables
// File normal.scad
// Based on OpenSCAD model to print out an arbitrary surface
// defined as z = f(x,y)
// First used in "3D Printed Science Projects"
//(2016, first volume)
// Either prints the surface as two sided and variable
// thick = thickness
// Or if thick = 0, prints a top surface with a flat bottom

overall_scale = 100;
SDx = 36.0; //Standard deviation, x variable
SDy = 36.0; // Standard deviation, y variable
meanX= 100.0; //Mean of the x variable
meanY = 100.0; // Mean of the y variable
```

```
corrCoeff - 0; // -1 < corrCoeff < 1
scale = 10*200*200; //scaling factor
add_base = 4; // additional base thickness, mm
denom = 1 - pow (corrCoeff, 2);

// Constant in front of exponential part of equation
const = scale/ (2. * PI * SDx * SDy * sqrt (denom) );

// probability density function
function f(x, y) =
   add_base * 199 / overall_scale + const *
   exp ( -(1 / (2 * denom) ) *
  ( pow( (x - meanX) / SDx, 2) +
    pow( (y-meanY) / SDy, 2) -
    2 * corrCoeff * (x - meanX) * (y - meanY) / (SDx * SDy) )
   );

thick = 0; //set to 0 for flat bottom
           //else is thickness of print
xmax = 199;
ymax = 199;

toppoints = (xmax + 1) * (ymax + 1);

center = [xmax / 2, ymax / 2];

points = concat(
    [for(y = [0:ymax], x = [0:xmax]) [x, y, f(x, y)]],
// top face
   (thick ? //bottom face
      [for(y = [0:ymax], x = [0:xmax])
      [x, y, f(x, y) - thick * 199 / overall_scale]]
    :
      [for(y = [0:ymax], x = [0:xmax]) [x, y, 0]]
   )
);

zbounds = [min([for(i = points) i[2]]),
           max([for(i = points) i[2]])];

function quad(a, b, c, d, r = false) = r ?
   [[a, b, c], [c, d, a]]
 :
   [[c, b, a], [a, d, c]]
; //create triangles from quad
```

```
faces = concat(
    [for(bottom = [0, toppoints], i = [for(x = [0:xmax - 1],
    y = [0:ymax - 1]) //build top and bottom
        quad(
            x + (xmax + 1) * (y + 1) + bottom,
            x + (xmax + 1) * y + bottom,
            x + 1 + (xmax + 1) * y + bottom,
            x + 1 + (xmax + 1) * (y + 1) + bottom,
            bottom
        )], v = i) v],
    [for(i = [for(x = [0, xmax], y = [0:ymax - 1])
    //build left and right
        quad(
            x + (xmax + 1) * y + toppoints,
            x + (xmax + 1) * y,
            x + (xmax + 1) * (y + 1),
            x + (xmax + 1) * (y + 1) + toppoints,
            x
        )], v = i) v],
    [for(i = [for(x = [0:xmax - 1], y = [0, ymax])
        //build front and back
        quad(
            x + (xmax + 1) * y + toppoints,
            x + 1 + (xmax + 1) * y+ toppoints,
            x + 1 + (xmax + 1) * y,
            x + (xmax + 1) * y,
            y
        )], v = i) v]
);

scale(overall_scale / 199) rotate([90, 0, 0]) polyhedron(points, faces);
// End model
```

What happens if ρ is not zero? Then the variables x and y are correlated and clustering around a line. That means that the probability distribution will start to develop a spike or fin, since since the total probability has to be constant, and thus the volume will stay constant. Figure 6-3 and 6-4 show two views of the same case as Figure 6-2, but with $\rho = 0.7$. Notice the angling of the "fin" when ρ is not zero.

Figure 6-3. *Normal distribution: standard deviation in front to back direction is three times that from side to side, $\rho = 0.7$*

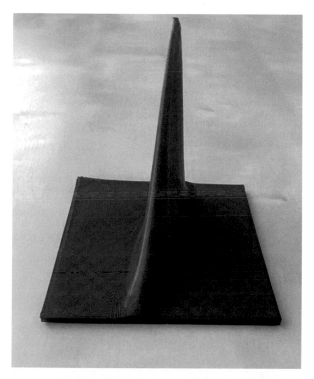

Figure 6-4. *Same as in Figure 6-3, but viewed from the side*

Finally, in Figure 6-5, we have these three cases side by side. Notice that the "fin" starts climbing up as the distribution begins to cluster around a linear relationship between the two variables.

Figure 6-5. *x and y with equal means and standard deviations and ρ = 0 (left); same but with one standard deviation three times that of the other (center); and same as the center, but with ρ = 0.7 (right).*

Printing the Model

This model can be scaled in various ways to make it easier to print, or to make it fit on your printer. By default, it creates a model that is 100 × 100 mm in the *x-y* plane. The variable overall_scale controls this. You can also add a base under the distribution to avoid having the tails of the distribution get too thin. The variable add_base (defaulted to 4 mm) controls this thickness. You can see this added base at the bottom of the distribution in Figure 6-1. The parameter scale controls the height of the peak of the distribution.

If you want to have your distribution roughly in the center of the model, then make the xmean and ymean variables each equal to 100. The models shown in Figures 6-1 through 6-5 have means of 100 and standard deviations of either 36 or 12.

The models are created so that one edge touches the platform. This produces a smoother curve with less of a stair-step effect caused by the layers of the print in areas where the surface is nearly horizontal. The symmetrical model (Figure 6-1) was printed this way. However, if the "fin" starts to get bigger, you may want to rotate the model about its *x* or *y* axis so that it prints fin-up to reduce overhangs that might make the print likely to break loose from the platform or require support structures.

If you want to have a hollow model, change the parameter thick to something other than zero. The program will then create a hollow model with a surface thick mm deep. In this case, you probably want to print the model on edge because otherwise not enough of the model may be touching the platform. Be careful doing this, though, because in order to keep the shape of the surface correct on both sides, the thick variable only increases thickness along the *z* axis, and steep sides of a function may result in areas that will look fine in the preview and the STL, but will result in holes in the print because they are too thin to reproduce.

Combinations and Pascal's Triangle

If I have three things and I want to figure out how many combinations of two of them there are, I could just figure it out. However, it gets a little more complicated to know how many combinations there are if we have 100 things and want to choose 22 of them. Fortunately there is a formula for that; it is often referred to as **n choose k**, or in our case, 3 choose 2 or 100 choose 22. It is written like this:

$$\binom{n}{k} = n! / \left(k!(n-k)! \right)$$

where *n!* is *n factorial*. The factorial of a whole number is the product of the number and all the positive whole numbers less than it. Or you can write this:

$$n! = n * (n - 1)!$$

You will notice this is *recursive*—we define factorial in terms of a factorial. *0!* is defined as being equal to 1, and we stop counting down at 0.

So, 3 choose 2 is 3! / (2! * (3 − 2)!), which works out to (3 * 2 * 1 * 1) / ((2 * 1 * 1) * (1 * 1)) = 3, giving us three ways to pick two things out of three options. To check this, imagine we have three blocks labeled *A*, *B*, and *C*. The options are *AB*, *AC*, and *BC* (assuming the order does not matter, and that you cannot choose a block twice). On the other hand, 100 choose 22 would be 100! / (22! * 78!), which is roughly a 7 with 21 zeroes after it.

Our new friend *n* choose *k* has another name, too: the *binomial coefficient*. It pops up in many situations in math besides probability, and you can read about many of them by searching in Wikipedia for "binomial coefficient." One way of visualizing the binomial coefficients is called *Pascal's triangle*, after Blaise Pascal (1623–1662); search for "Pascal's triangle" in Wikipedia for a good overview. The rows of the triangle are values of *n*, and the columns are *k*.

The Model

We have created a 3D printed model of Pascal's triangle (Figure 6-6 and Listing 6-2). In Figure 6-6, **n = 0** and **k = 0** are the single square at the far left (0 choose 0 works out to have a value of 1). Then the next row is 1 choose 0 (also 1) and 1 choose 1 (also 1). Things get more interesting in subsequent rows, as shown in Figure 6-6.

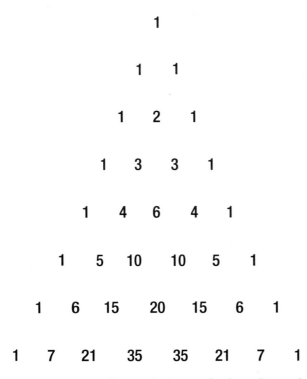

Figure 6-6. *Pascal's triangle, for n = 0 (top) to 8 (bottom)*

As you can infer from the example in Figure 6-6, the values get very big very fast after 7 or 8 rows. Figure 6-7 shows a 3D printed model of *n = 0 to 7*. As you can see from Figure 6-6, the values of each row entry are the sum of the two entries in the previous row (with zeroes where there is no entry.)

The number of rows is set with the parameter numRows. Because the count starts at zero, numRows = 7 prints out a model with 8 rows. Figure 6-7 shows the 3D printed model for eight rows (the same as Figure 6-6). It blows up pretty fast after that.

Figure 6-7. *Pascal's triangle model (n = 0, k = 0 at lower left corner)*

■ **Note** There is a sort of "3D Pascal's triangle" (called ***Pascal's pyramid*** or ***Pascal's tetrahedron***), but that is not what we created here. We would have needed a fourth dimension (or some other way to independently show position and numerical value) for that! You might consider how to represent Pascal's pyramid in pieces or as a series of models. Wikipedia has a good write-up under "Pascal's pyramid."

Printing the Model

The relative size of the squares along the rows and columns are scalable with the parameter boxsize, which is the length of the size of the box along the row and column dimensions. These two dimensions need to be the same to avoid distorting the pyramid. The vertical dimension can be scaled independently though with the parameter zsize. If you scale the model in your slicing software, be careful to scale consistently at least in the *x*- and *y*-axes.

The peaks in the *z* direction (the *n* choose *k* values) can get big quickly. If you have a large and skinny tower on this print, you may want to print two at the same time or print a ***cooling tower*** when you print it. A ***cooling tower*** is just a cylinder that you print at the same time as something tall and skinny. It moves the print head off your print long enough for the previous layer to cool and avoids having the tall, skinny piece come out blobby (instead of the clean point you want).

Listing 6-2. Pascal's Triangle Model

```
// Pascal's triangle
// File pascal.scad
// This make one triangle
// Because of minimum cooling time issues, we recommend
// also printing a cooling tower or a second set of this print

numRows = 7; //number of rows minus 1
    // value of 7 gives 8 rows
function oddOffset(row) = row;
boxsize = 6; //multiplier in x and y directions, mm
zsize = 2; //multiplier in z direction,mm

//recursive factorial function
//from OpenSCAD documentation example
function factorial(n) = n == 0 ? 1 : factorial(n - 1) * n;

// n choose k function
function nchoosek(n, k) = factorial (n) /
    (factorial(k) * factorial (n-k) );

for(y = [0:numRows], x = [0:y]) {
    union()
    translate([boxsize*(x-y/2), boxsize*y,0])
    cube([boxsize,boxsize,zsize*nchoosek(y,x)]);
}
// end model
```

Rolling Dice

The earliest exposure most of us have to random numbers is flipping a coin or playing a game where we roll dice. One of the things we assume when we do either of those things is that any outcome is equally likely, be it heads or tails for the coin, and one through six for a die. This is called a ***uniform distribution***. If we plotted the probability of rolling any given number on a die, we would just get a flat line from one to six.

Rolling Multiple Identical Dice

It gets a little more interesting if we throw two dice, or throw one die twice and take the output as the sum of the two throws. Now the outcome 1 becomes impossible, and we have new outcomes (7 through 12) that now are possible. It turns out that if you figure out all the ways to get a sum of 2, 3, 4, and so on, the probability distribution is triangular in shape. If you figure it out for three, four, five, and six dice, gradually the outcome starts to trend toward the normal distribution that we discuss earlier in this chapter. We thought it would be fun to use the third dimension to show this progression, so we created a model for it, shown in Listing 6-3.

Listing 6-3. Dice Probability

```
//A model of the probability distributions of throwing
//different combinations of dice
//File diceProbability.scad

base = .6; //added base piece for stability
size = [3, 10, 100]; //dimensions of the model
// if the following line is uncommented, shows
// one 12 sided die vs 2, 6 sided ones, etc
//dice = [[1, 12], [2, 6], [3, 4], [4, 3], [6, 2]];

// if the following line is uncommented, shows results for
// six-sided dice- first one (uniform), then two (triangle),
dice = [[1, 6], [2, 6], [3, 6], [4, 6], [5, 6]];

//accumulation function
function sum(a, i = 0) = (i >= len(a)) ? 0 :
   a[i] + sum(a, i + 1);

function count(a, n, i = 0) = (i >= len(a)) ? 0 :
   ((a[i] == n) ? 1 : 0) + count(a, n, i + 1);

module distribution(n = 2, d = 6) {
   combinations = [for(i = [0:pow(d, n) - 1])
      [for(j= [0:n - 1]) (floor(i / pow(d, j)) % d) + 1]];
   totals = [for(i = combinations) sum(i)];
   distribution = [for(i = [0:d * n]) count(totals, i)];
   echo(distribution);
   for(i = [0:d * n]) translate([i, 0, 0])
      cube([1.0001, 1.0001,
      distribution[i] / (pow(d, n)) + base / size[2]]);
}

// scale the output
scale(size) for(i = [0: len(dice)]) translate([0, i, 0])
distribution(dice[i][0], dice[i][1]);
// end model
```

Figures 6-8 and 6-9 show two views of what happens for one through five six-sided dice. You can see the uniform distribution for one die for outcomes from 1 through 6, with zero probability of rolling a 0.

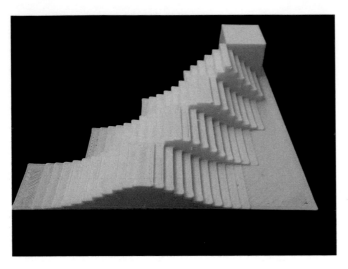

Figure 6-8. *From farthest to closest, probability distributions of the sums of the outcome of rolling one through five dice. Outcomes go from 0 at the right to 30 at the left. (There is no way to roll a 0, of course, but the program starts computing there.)*

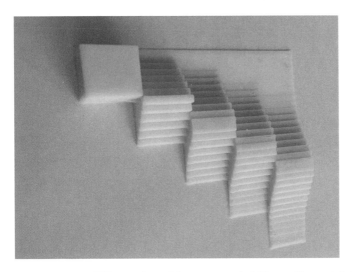

Figure 6-9. *A different view of the same probability as Figure 6-8. Outcomes go from 0 at the top to 30 at the bottom, one die at the left and five at the right.*

By the time we get to five dice (closest to you in Figure 6-8) we are approaching a normal distribution. In Figure 6-8, we wanted to show the more interesting distribution in front. This works out to looking at the progression of probability of rolling a 0 at the far right and of a 30 at the far left.

Rolling Combinations of Different Dice

We also wanted to ask a different question: if you have one 12-sided die, how is the probability of any given number coming up any different than if you had, say, three four-sided dice? The answer to that is in Figure 6-10 (yes, it is). In retrospect, of course, it's obvious that in this case as well some numbers are not possible when you are adding the results of multiple dice rolls. The distribution here, too, is moving away from a uniform one to as close as it can get (given the limitations of the stated problem) to a normal one.

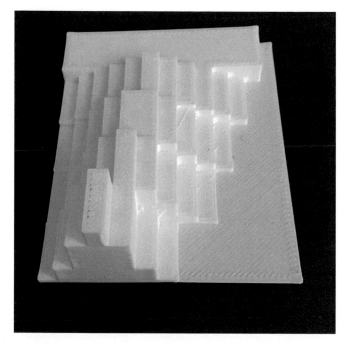

Figure 6-10. *Probability of rolling 0 through 12 (again, 0 is at the right and 12 at the left) with one 12-sided die (farthest back, at the top, uniform) through the sum of six two-sided dice (coin flips), nearest you.*

■ **Note** Probability theory's *central limit theorem* says if you add random numbers (with some constraints), the probability of their sums will approach a normal distribution. A closely related distribution for continuous variables (unlike dice rolls, which are discrete variables, because you only get outcomes 1, 2, 3 … and not 1.1, 1.2, and so on) is called the *Irwin-Hall distribution*. If you have some calculus background, you might explore that as well.

DICE IN ROLE-PLAYING GAMES

If you have never played a role-playing game like Dungeons and Dragons, you might wonder who would use anything other than six-sided dice. However, there are many strategy games in which part of the game play involves an element of luck. In this type of game, players take on the role of a character (often some sort of medieval or fantasy warrior) and "fight" using rolls of dice to see who comes out alive and/or unscathed.

In these games dice are referred to using the letter *d* followed by the number of sides, so a 6-sided die would be referred to as a *d6*, and a 20-sided die would be a *d20*. If you are rolling multiple dice and adding the results (as is often the case when calculating how much damage a weapon or spell does, or how much damage is healed by a healing spell), you put that number before the *d*, so 3d6 means roll three six-sided dice and total up the values. A common set of dice used for such a game includes a d4, a d6, a d8, a d10, a d12, a d20, and usually a d100 or "decader," which is also 10-sided, but has multiples of 10 on the faces, and is used in conjunction with a d10 to simulate a 100-sided die. There are even some obscure cases where the rules call for a d3, a d2, or even a d1. You would not actually roll a d1 of course—the outcome is just a certainty.

In "d20" systems like Dungeons and Dragons or Pathfinder Roleplaying Game, a d20 is used for attacks in combat, when attempting to use a skill like Stealth or Diplomacy, or to try to avoid the effects of some magical spells. If a weapon or spell does damage to a monster, the player then rolls a number of smaller dice to determine how much damage is done. These probability distributions become interesting when deciding whether your character should use, for instance, a greatsword that does 2d6 points of damage or a greataxe that does 1d12 points of damage.

A fighter choosing a weapon has some math to do when deciding which weapon to use. While the maximums are the same, the sword does 7 points of damage on average while the axe's average is only 6.5, and the sword's minimum damage is one point higher. The interesting thing, though, is that the axe has a 1/12 probability of doing the maximum damage (and an equal probability of doing the minimum damage, or any other possible value), whereas the sword's probability distribution is weighted much more heavily toward the center, making it six times as likely to do the average damage (7) as to do the maximum damage. A fighter who chooses the greatsword is taking more chances and will do damage on the high and low ends of the scale more often than the one with the greatsword, who will do roughly average damage most of the time. The prints in this section explore how some of these possible combinations of dice compare.

Rich is a big fan of these games, and we embarked on these models in part because of his curiosity about how the probability distributions differed. Figure 6-11 shows his set of dice, from a 4-sided die through a 20-sided one. Rich ordered these, 3D printed in metal, from the 3D printing service bureau Shapeways.com. The four-sided die in the lower left is Rich's design, and the others are from the Pinwheel Dice Set with Decader set by Chuck Stover, aka "ceramicwombat" (www.shapeways.com/ product/DKP3VVFL8/pinwheel-dice-set-with-decader?optionId=43314776).

Figure 6-11. *Different-sided dice*

The Multiple-Dice Model

This model solves the problem of computing the probability distributions created by rolling various dice combinations by what engineers call a ***brute force*** method. That is, it calculates all the possible combinations and adds up how many combinations give a particular result. The model starts with an array, ***dice***, like this:

```
dice = [[1, 12], [2, 6], [3, 4], [4, 3], [6, 2]];
```

Each entry in the array is ***[number of dice, number of sides]***—so, the preceding example would compute the probability distribution created by rolling a single 12-sided die, the next of two 6-sided dice, and so on. You can graph as many situations as you like (and as will fit on your printer).

The other parameters you have to work with are base and the size arrays. The value of base (in mm) is how thick a layer will be drawn under all the distributions. It is 0.6 mm in this version. This prevents low probabilities that would be less than one layer tall from disappearing in the print and makes the zero-probability values visible (which also prevents the model from being broken into disconnected islands). The size array gives the dimensions of the width of each "basket" in the graph, the width of each graph, and a multiplier for the probability numbers—in other words, scaling factors in x, y, and z.

THINKING ABOUT THESE MODELS: LEARNING LIKE A MAKER

This chapter came about partly as the result of a discussion about the outcomes of various dice rolls—more or less the questions that are answered with our multiple-dice models. Rich was interested in optimizing his role-playing adventures, and Joan had always found probability rather counterintuitive. Creating these 3D models really built our insights as we went.

As we have noticed frequently, textbooks on probability treat multivariate cases as advanced topics, but in many ways the manipulations of the data are more intuitive and physical than the single-variable cases.

We looked up various ways of deriving some of the models in this chapter and were struck by how much complicated algebra or use of calculus was used to explain concepts that are not actually all that complex. We approached the dice probability models as brute-force calculations to avoid needing to delve too much into mathematics that some readers have not seen before. The brute force method is also more useful for showing how the probability distributions arise naturally from the physical act of rolling dice.

Where to Learn More

The ideas in this chapter underlie many different concepts in probability and statistics. The most obvious thing to try would be to create a model based on actual data. Formulas for calculating the mean, standard deviation and correlation coefficient are available in links we have given as we have gone along. You might need to offset and/or scale your data so that the mean is about 100 in order that you fit within the model.

■ **Caution**   Analyzing data that has more complex correlations than the simple linear relationships presumed by our models is a big topic all of its own, beyond the scope of both our models and what we can cover here. If you are creating 3D prints to visualize the probability distributions of real data, be sure that your data fits the assumptions here and be sure you understand how the scaling algorithms work.

We have given Wikipedia references as we went along, or at least the right word(s) to search in Wikipedia. Other good resources for learning more about probability are available at the Khan Academy (www.khanacademy.org), which has many videos and practice exercises. Its interactive exercises for building intuition about the correlation coefficient would be a very good complement to creating the first models in this chapter. Similarly, the Math Is Fun site has a good discussion of correlation and very lucid directions about computing some of the parameters we have used in this chapter. You can find that site's take on this at www.mathsisfun.com/data/correlation.html.

If you want more sophisticated discussions with detailed equations for general problems, Wolfram Mathworld comes at the correlation coefficient differently than we did here. It is worth a read particularly if you are going to derive these parameters from data or if you are looking at teaching a college-level course. The relevant information can be found at http://mathworld.wolfram.com/CorrelationCoefficient.html.

Teaching with These Models

Teachers may find themselves bringing probability into data analysis at various junctures in math and science. If you are teaching in high school in the United States, the NGSS science teaching standards discuss probability as a tool, for example under HS-LS3-3 "Inheritance and variation of traits" (www.nextgenscience.org/dci-arrangement/hs-ls3-heredity-inheritance-and-variation-traits.). Using statistics and probability to make sense of data applies with varying degrees of sophistication as students analyze data and try to make sense of anomalies.

When we looked through the (U.S.) Common Core math teaching standards, we found that probability is nominally covered at the high school level (www.corestandards.org/Math/Content/HSS/introduction/) and correlation (www.corestandards.org/Math/Content/8/SP/A/1/) and related topics in the eighth grade.

At the college level or for the general public, we think these models may be very helpful as classroom discussion pieces or perhaps as pieces for exhibits or outreach presentations. Perhaps there are some fun museum exhibits in here somewhere!

Project Ideas

These models might be useful ways of displaying hypothetical or actual data to visualize outcomes if two variables have particular means, standard deviations, and correlation coefficients. Very often statistical data is difficult for people to understand in the abstract. In other words, the models in this chapter might provide a way of displaying the results of other experiments in a way that encourages participation and discussion, or of doing some what-if displays to think about what particular outcomes might imply. (As we noted in an earlier caution, though, be sure you understand how you are scaling each of your variables.)

If you are a role-playing game fan, perhaps you can systematically build on Rich's sidebar to figure out the optimal probability for various strategies in your favorite game. Or maybe there are ways to take these hypothetical gaming strategies and see if you can create and test a hypothesis about how similar strategies might be playing out in small, contained ecosystems.

To go beyond the models here, you might want to think of other ways to use the visualization of the binomial coefficients (Pascal's triangle) by considering other places the binomial coefficients come up both in discussing possible combinations of objects (as we talked about with n choose k earlier in the chapter) and also in some formulas that can make complex algebra simpler. Searching on "binomial coefficient" will let you see some of the algebraic applications, which are elegant but a little complex and off-topic here.

Summary

In this chapter we create models of various probability distributions. First we create the normal (bell curve) distribution for two variables and explored how the models changed when we altered the standard deviations of the variables and the correlation coefficient relating them. Next we look at combination problems and create a model of Pascal's triangle, with a short excursion to talk about binomial coefficients. Finally, we make models of what happens if we roll progressively more dice and visualize the transition from a uniform distribution (with one die) to a nearly normal one.

CHAPTER 7

■ ■ ■

Digital Logic

Computers are made up of what can be thought of as tiny switches that are either on or off, and therefore can only process ones and zeros. If you represent **on** as the number 1 and **off** as the number 0, you are left with the problem of figuring out a way to calculate using one ones and zeros. Computer scientists solved this problem by doing calculations in *binary* (base 2) arithmetic, which uses only the digits 0 and 1 to represent any number, just as our familiar base 10 arithmetic uses the digits 0 through 9. Search online for tutorials on "binary arithmetic" to learn more about this—we like one at the Khan Academy (www.khanacademy.org/math/algebra-home/alg-intro-to-algebra/algebra-alternate-number-bases/v/number-systems-introduction) and also this one: http://ryanstutorials.net/binary-tutorial/binary-arithmetic.php.

The second problem computer designers needed to solve was how to create a mix of hardware and software to control how data flows through the computer. They did that with *logic gates*—components that take binary inputs and perform Boolean operations on them. **Boolean** operations take one or more binary inputs and create one binary output, and logic gates are the physical devices that do these operations (the "tiny switches" we mentioned in the previous paragraph)..In this chapter, we create simple models of logic gates that you can use to learn about the basic components of computer logic.

Logic Gates

A computer chip may be composed of millions of logic gates packaged together. You can represent a circuit of any complexity by just few types of gates, one of which have just one input, the rest of which have two. Some logic gates are combinations of other gates.

Types of Logic Gates

The one-input gate is the NOT gate, which flips its input (a 1 becomes a 0, and a 0 becomes a 1). As you will see, the NOT prefix in general does this flipping function when applied to other gates that follow (such as AND and NAND).

© Joan Horvath and Rich Cameron 2017
J. Horvath and R. Cameron, *3D Printed Science Projects Volume 2*,
DOI 10.1007/978-1-4842-2695-7_7

All the other gates have two inputs:

- The AND gate outputs a 1 if both of its inputs are 1. Otherwise, it outputs a 0.

- The NAND (short for "NOT AND") gate negates the output of an AND gate.

- The OR gate outputs a 1 if either (or both) of its inputs are 1.

- The NOR ("NOT OR") gate outputs a 1 only if both inputs are 0 (negates an OR gate).

- The XOR gate ("exclusive OR," pronounced "ex-or") outputs a 1 if exactly one of its inputs is 1.

- The XNOR ("exclusive NOT OR") outputs a 1 if both inputs are 0 or both inputs are 1 (negates XOR).

If we collect these inputs and outputs in tabular form, the result is called a *truth table* (shown in Table 7-1).

Table 7-1. *Truth Table for Two-Input Gates*

Inputs		Gate Outputs					
		AND	NAND	OR	NOR	XOR	XNOR
0	0	0	1	0	1	0	1
0	1	0	1	1	0	1	0
1	0	0	1	1	0	1	0
1	1	1	0	1	0	0	1

■ **Note** It is possible to create all the other gates out of a combination of all NOR gates or all NAND gates. This was discovered by Charles Sanders Peirce in the 1880s but was not published until 1933, years after he died. For that reason, the NOR gate is sometimes called *Peirce's arrow.* There are also other equivalencies that involve using the "NOT" of the gate's inputs, called *De Morgan equivalents.* For example, the AND gate is the same as an OR gate with its outputs and inputs all negated. We experiment with a few of these when we build some logic circuits later in the chapter.

Physical Gate Components

Electrically switched logic components have been around for about 80 years. Claude Shannon worked on an early computing machine using electrical switches for gates at MIT in the late 1930s, and later worked at Bell Labs. The invention of the vacuum tube and then the transistor allowed for gates to be made smaller and smaller as those components shrank.

Currently you can buy computer chips with many logic gates. Field-programmable gated arrays (FPGAs) allow different types of gates to be enabled on a chip by software, for maximum flexibility.

It is difficult to purchase individual gates as a consumer. We found one particular chip that has 8 gates and sells for about 39 cents if you buy one at a time. Creating a demonstrator with a physical chip that correctly handles an input and output for one component is tricky, as we discuss in the next section.

Abstract Representations

The gates have standard representations in logic diagrams. Figure 7-1 shows our representation in the model. In a diagram, they are not normally labeled "AND" and "NOR" and so on—just the outline shape is shown.

By convention, inverting gates (NOT, NAND, NOR, and XNOR) have a circle on their output side (the top, as arranged in Figure 7-1). The exclusive OR gates (XOR, XNOR) have a double bar on their input side.

The colors in Figure 7-1 are not significant and were just chosen to make finding pieces easier when you have created a lot of them, without having excessive numbers of spools of filament on the go.

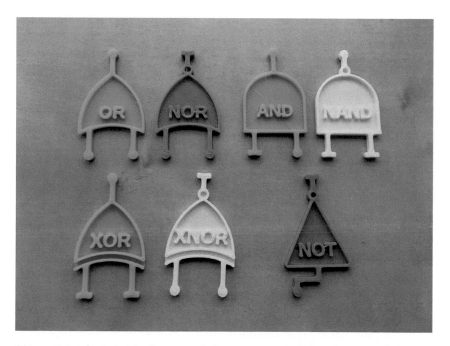

Figure 7-1. *The individual gate symbols, as we represent them in our models*

■ **Note**   In a real electronic gate, the input would have either a high or low voltage, which would be interpreted as 1 or **on**, or 0 or **off**, respectively. Here we have static models with a bar-shaped end to show a 1 and a circle on the end to show a 0. The NOT gate in Figure 7-1, for example, has an input (on the bottom) of 0 and an output (top) of 1.

The Model

Real electronic gates change the state of their inputs and outputs based on electrical signals flowing through them. This means that a realistic model somehow has to mimic electrical energy flowing through wires. We wanted a purely mechanical—and preferably very simple—model instead that would capture the behaviors of gates (and circuits made up of them) while not requiring any actual flowing of electricity or electronic components.

■ **Caution**   If you print them at the default size used for this chapter, some of these parts are very small. They should be kept away from young children and not used as toys.

Gates

We wanted to create a very simple model for each gate. The way we did that was to create all the possible combinations of input and output for each gate and then use them like pieces of a jigsaw puzzle to create circuits. Figure 7-2 shows all the possible combinations of input and output for NOR and NAND gates. The other gates (except NOT) have similar sets of four options per gate. NOT just has two—one for each input.

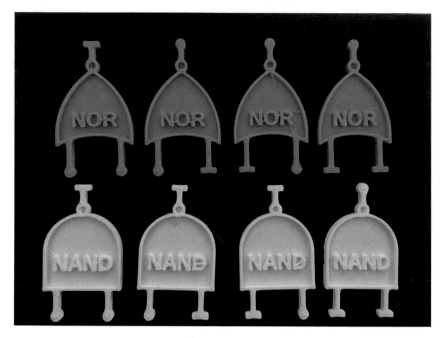

Figure 7-2. *The full set of NAND and NOR gates*

To put it another way, we made the truth tables visible in plastic parts. As noted earlier, a round input or output should be interpreted as 0 or *off*, and a bar-shaped one as 1 or *on*. Although this creates a lot of pieces, it has the virtue of being extremely simple to print and very tactile and visual.

Wires

The next challenge was to figure out how to connect these pieces to each other. We created several different types of connectors, or *wires*, as we will refer to them from here on. The model creates both the types of wire that have connections for zeros and connections for ones.

Side Connection Wires

The first type of wire is shown in Figure 7-3. The model allows just one input, which can be branched into many outputs. In Figure 7-3, the outputs are on the bottom of the pieces as pictured, and the inputs on the top. Since each wire is connecting outputs that are a 1 only to inputs of another gate that are also 1, and similarly only 0 to 0, the connectors only need to connect circles (zeros) to circles and bars (ones) to bars.

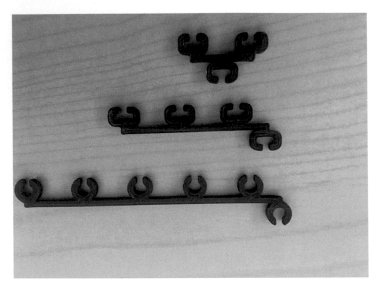

Figure 7-3. *The simple connectors (different for 0 and 1 terminations). The model refers to these as side wires.*

The wires can have an arbitrary number of outputs, and the outputs can be on both sides of the input. To simplify specifying the number of outputs desired, the number passed to the `wires` module only specifies the number of connectors on one side of the input.

The sign of the number is used to specify whether there should be a connector on the other side as well, so to include a (single) connector on the other side, a negative number is used. The absolute value of the number of connections is how many connectors are to the left of the input connection in Figure 7-3. So, from top to bottom, these are a –1 wire, a 3 wire, and a 5 wire.

Back Wires and Risers

We realized we needed *feedback* wires—connections that go from the output of one gate back to the input of another. These are shown in Figure 7-4.

Figure 7-4. *The feedback wires, different ones for 0 and 1 terminations, shown here with (top) and without (bottom) risers that allow crossing. The model refers to these as back wires and the risers as risers. For scale, an AND gate is shown with an attached riser.*

We also created *risers,* spacers that can be used to elevate one wire above another in case our wires need to cross each other. Figure 7-4 shows one feedback wire with risers and one without. The risers can be stacked if necessary.

Connecting Wires

Finally, we need to represent just a wire carrying a signal, as well as a way to show an input or an output signal coming into our little systems. We created the pieces in Figure 7-5 for a wire carrying a 0 or 1.

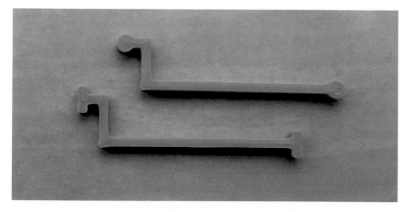

Figure 7-5. *Input/output pieces for 0 (top) and 1 (bottom) input or output signals. The model refers to these as forward wires.*

Just Drawing on Paper

The other way to connect up a circuit is to use the gates and just draw the connections between them on a piece of paper, using a different color marker for 1 and 0. You can, for example, use blue for 1 and red for 0. We show an example of this when we create an adder circuit later in the chapter.

Printing the Pieces

Listing 7-3 shows the model for all the pieces, both gates and wires. The model is designed so that you can export an STL with a complete set of one gate (all the possible combinations of inputs and outputs) or a specified set of wires.

To print a particular gate, you remove the *!* from the piece you do *not* want to print (gates or wires). OpenSCAD has a convention that something with a *!* in front of it is the only routine that should be called. Thus, we remove a *!* to disable printing whichever we do *not* want to create (gates or wires). The changes are detailed in the following list:

- To print a particular gate:

    - Disable the printing of wires by removing the *!* from `!wires(side,5)`.

    - Change `!gates(none)` to `!gates(name of the gate)`, for example `!gates(or)`.

- To print a particular type of wire (see captions for Figures 7-3 through 7-5 for options):

    - Disable the printing of gates by removing the *!* from `!gates(none)`.

    - Change the `!wires(side, 5)` to `!wires(name of the type of wire, parameter)`, for example `!wires(side, -5)`.

If you are printing `forward` or `back` wires, the parameter does not do anything. It is only used for the `side` wires.

■ **Note** If your wires and gates have trouble fitting into each other, you can adjust the `clearance` variable up a little or increase the `size` variable (which will make everything bigger).

Listing 7-1. Circuit Model

```
// Model of logic gates and connectors
// File gates.scad
// Rich "Whosawhatsis" Cameron, March 2017
// Create logic gates with all permutations of inputs and outputs
```

```
// A "1" or "TRUE" is a crossbar
// A "0" or "FALSE" is circle
// And connectors, input, and output pieces

size = 30; //Scaling in mm - roughly bounding box of gate symbols

thick = 1; //Line thickness; connector lines are twice this
height = 3; //Max height above platform of gates, mm
fontsize = size / 5;
fontweight = thick;

clearance = .4; // Parameter governing clearance of parts
                // that fit into each other

// Remove the "!" from the piece you do NOT want to print
// (gates or wires)

// To make a set of gates,
// Replace "none" with one of the names of gates
// listed later in the model.
// All possible permutations of inputs and outputs
// for that gate are printed. The optional second parameter
// "rows" determines how many rows these will be split
// into on the printer platform.

!gates(none);

// Or, for wires, replace the first parameter of "wires"
// with one of the types of wires named later in the model
// to print a set of those wires.
// The second parameter is the number of connection points.
// Negative numbers have connections on two sides
!wires(side, -5);

//gates
none = 0;
or = 1;
xor = 2;
and = 3;
not = 4;
nor = 5;
xnor = 6;
nand = 7;

//wires
side = 0; //connectors branching sideways
forward = 1; // data input, with a 1 or 0
back = 2; //feedback wires
riser = 3; //offsets two layers
```

```
$fs = .2;
$fa = 2;

// gates makes multiple instances of objects define by gate
// second parameter is how many are in a row
module gates(type, row = 2) {
    if(type == not) for(i = [0:1]) translate([
        (size + 2) * (i % row),
        (size + 15) * floor(i / row),
        0
    ]) gate(type, [i]);
    else if(type == none) wire(forward);
    else for(i = [0:3]) translate([
        (size + 2) * (i % row),
        (size + 14) * floor(i / row),
        0
    ]) gate(type, [floor(i / 2), i % 2]);
}

// Module gate makes the gates
module gate(type, in = [0, 0]) for(h = [0, height - 1]) {
    linear_extrude(height = h + 1, convexity = 5) {
        if(type % 4 == or) {
            _or(in, h ? thick : 0);
            _out(
                xor(in[0] || in[1],
                type >= not),
                h ? thick : 0,
                (type >= not) ? true : false
            );
            translate([0, -size * .15, 0])
                offset(fontweight/2 - fontsize * .075) text(
                    (type >= not) ? "NOR" : "OR", size = fontsize,
                    halign = "center",
                    valign = "center",
                    font = ":style=Bold"
                );
        }
        else if(type % 4 == xor) {
            _xor(in, h ? thick : 0);
            _out(
                xor(xor(in[0], in[1]), type >= not),
                h ? thick : 0,
                (type >= not) ? true : false
            );
```

```
            translate([0, -size * .08, 0])
                offset(fontweight/2 - fontsize * .075) text(
                    (type >= not) ? "XNOR" : "XOR",
                    size = fontsize,
                    halign = "center",
                    valign = "center",
                    font = ":style=Bold"
                );
        }
        else if(type % 4 == and) {
            _and(in, h ? thick : 0);
            _out(
                xor(in[0] && in[1], type >= not),
                h ? thick : 0,
                (type >= not) ? true : false
            );
            translate([0, -size * .15, 0])
                offset(fontweight/2 - fontsize * .075) text(
                    (type >= not) ? "NAND" : "AND",
                    size = fontsize,
                    halign = "center",
                    valign = "center",
                    font = ":style=Bold"
                );
        }
        else if(type % 4 == none) {
            if(type == not) {
                _none(in, h ? thick : 0);
                _out(
                    xor(in[0], type >= not),
                    h ? thick : 0,
                    (type >= not) ? true : false
                );
                translate([0, -size * .25, 0])
                    offset(fontweight/2 - fontsize * .075) text(
                        (type >= not) ? "NOT" : "",
                        size = fontsize,
                        halign = "center",
                        valign = "center",
                        font = ":style=Bold"
                    );
            } else _forwardwire([in[0]], h ? thick : 0);
        }
    }
}
```

```
module wires(type, value = 1) {
   if(type == side) wire(type, [(value < 1) ? 1 : 0, abs(value)]);
   else wire(type);
}

module wire(type, w = [0, 1]) {
   if(type == side) {
      linear_extrude(height = height, convexity = 5) for(i = [0, 1])
         translate(
            i * [-size * 2 / 3 * (w[1]) - thick,
            -thick * 4,
            0
         ]) rotate(i * 180) _crosswire([i], thick, w = w);
   } else if(type == forward) {
      linear_extrude(height = height, convexity = 5) for(i = [0, 1])
         translate(i * [-size / 3 - thick * 7, 0, 0]) rotate(i * 180)
            _forwardwire([i], thick);
   } else if(type == back) {
      linear_extrude(height = height, convexity = 5) for(i = [0, 1])
         translate(i * [-thick * 4, 10 + thick + 5, 0])
            _backwire([i], thick);
   } else if(type == riser) {
      for(i = [0, 1]) translate(i * [0, 0, 0]) rotate(i * 180)
         _wireriser([i], thick, height);
   }
}

// OpenSCAD doesn't have a built-in xor operator, so we need a
// function.
function xor(a, b) = (a || b) && !(a && b);

module _or(in = [0, 0], width = 0, l = 10) difference() {
   union() {
      if(l) _in(in, width, l = 1);
      difference() {
         intersection_for(i = [-1, 1])
            translate([i * size / 2, -size * .366, 0]) circle(size);
         translate([0, -size - size * .366, 0]) circle(size);
      }
   }
   if(width) offset(-width) _or(l = 0);
}

module _xor(in = [0, 0], width = 0, l = 10) difference() {
   union() {
      if(l) _in(in, width, l = 1);
      _or(l = 0);
   }
```

```
    if(width) union() {
        offset(-width) difference() {
            _or(l = 0);
            translate([0, -size - size * .366, 0])
                circle(size + width * 3);
        }
        translate([0, -size - size * .366, 0]) difference() {
            circle(size + width * 3);
            circle(size + width);
        }
    }
}

module _and(in = [0, 0], width = 0, l = 10) difference() {
    union() {
        if(l) _in(in, width, l = l);
        hull() {
            circle(size / 2);
            translate([-size / 2, -size / 2, 0])
                square([size, size / 4]);
        }
    }
    if(width) offset(-width) _and(l = 0);
}

// generic gate symbol (used for NOT)
module _none(in = [0], width = 0, l = 10) difference() {
    union() {
        if(l) _in(in, width, l = l);
        hull() {
            translate([0, size * .45, 0]) circle(size * .05);
            translate([-size * .45, -size * .45, 0]) circle(size * .05);
            translate([size * .45, -size * .45, 0]) circle(size * .05);
        }
    }
    if(width) offset(-width) _none(l - 0);
}

// Create connectors

module _forwardwire(in = [0], width = 0, l = 10) {
    for(i = [0:len(in) - 1]) translate([
        (len(in) > 1) ? size * 2 / 6 / (len(in) - 1) * i - size / 6 : 0,
        0,
        0
    ]) {
```

```
      _in(in, width, l = 1);
      _out(in[0], width, l = 1);
      square([width * 2, size], center = true);
   }
}

module _backwire(in = [0], width = 0, l = 10) {
   for(i = [0:len(in) - 1]) translate([
      (len(in) > 1) ? size * 2 / 6 / (len(in) - 1) * i - size / 6 : 0,
      0,
      0
   ]) {
      for(i = [0, 1]) rotate(180 * i) {
         translate([
            -size / 2,
            -size - l * 3,
            0
         ]) _out(in[0], width, l = 1);
         translate([-width, size / 2 + l * 3, 0])
            square([size / 2 + width * 2, width * 2]);
      }
      square([width * 2, size + l * 6], center = true);
   }
}

module _forwardwire(in = [0], width = 0, l = 10) {
   for(i = [0:len(in) - 1]) translate([
      (len(in) > 1) ? size * 2 / 6 / (len(in) - 1) * i - size / 6 : 0,
      0,
      0
   ]) {
      _in(in, width, l = 1);
      _out(in[0], width, l = 1);
      square([width * 2, size], center = true);
   }
}

module _crosswire(in = [0], width = 0, l = 10, w = [0, 0]) {
   for(side = [0, 1]) mirror([side, 0, 0]) if(w[side]) difference() {
      union() {
         translate([-width, -width, 0])
            square([
               size * 2 / 3 * (w[side] - .5) + width * 2,
               width * 2
            ]);
```

```
        for(i = [1:w[side]]) translate([
          size * 2 / 3 * (i - .5),
          0,
          0
        ]) {
          translate([0, 1 / 4, 0])
            square([width * 2, 1 / 2], center = true);
          translate([0, 1 / 2, 0]) offset(width * 2 + clearance)
            _end(in[0], width);
        }
        translate([0, -1 / 4, 0])
          square([width * 2, 1 / 2], center = true);
        translate([0, -1 / 2, 0]) offset(width * 2 + clearance)
          _end(in[0], width);
      }
      offset(clearance) {
        for(i = [1:w[side]]) translate([
          size * 2 / 3 * (i - .5),
          0,
          0
        ]) {
          translate([0, 1 / 2 + width * 2, 0])
            square([width * 2, width * 4], center = true);
          translate([0, 1 / 2, 0]) _end(in[0], width);
        }
        translate([0, -1 / 2 - width * 2, 0])
          square([width * 2, width * 4], center = true);
        translate([0, -1 / 2, 0]) _end(in[0], width);
      }
    }
  }
}

module _wireriser(in = [0], width = 0, h = height) {
  translate([0, -10, 0]) difference() {
    union() {
      linear_extrude(h + 2) offset(width * 2)
        _out(in[0], width, l = 0);
      linear_extrude(h * 2 + 2, convexity = 5) intersection() {
        offset(width * 2) _out(in[0], width, l = 0);
        translate([0, -width * 5, 0])
          _out(in[0], width, l = width * 5);
      }
    }
    translate([0, -width * 5, 0])
      linear_extrude(h * 2 + 2, center = true, convexity = 5)
        offset(clearance) _out(in[0], width, l = width * 5);
  }
}
```

131

```
module _in(in = [0], width = 0, l = 10) for(i = [0:len(in) - 1]) {
    translate([size * 2 / 3 * i - size / 3, 0, 0]) {
        if(len(in) > 1) translate([0, -size * .4 - l / 2, 0])
            square([width * 2, l + size * .2], center = true);
        else {
            translate([-width, -size / 2 - l / 2 - width, 0])
                square([size / 3 + width * 2, width * 2]);
            translate([size / 3, -size * .4, 0])
                square([width * 2, l + size * .2], center = true);
            translate([
                0,
                -size * .4 - l / 2 - (l / 2 + size * .2) / 2,
                0
            ]) square([width * 2, l / 2], center = true);
        }
        translate([0, -size / 2 - l, 0]) {
            _end(in[i], width);
        }
    }
}

module _out(out = 0, width = 0, inverting = false, l = 10) {
    difference() {
        union() {
            translate([0, size / 2 + l / 2 - .5, 0])
                square([width * 2, l + .5], center = true);
            translate([0, size / 2 + l, 0]) _end(out, width);
            if(inverting) translate([
                0,
                size * .5 - thick + thick * 2.5,
                0
            ]) circle(thick * 2.5);
        }
        if(width) offset(-width) _out(inverting = inverting, l = 0);
    }
}

module _end(on = true, width = 0) {
    if(on) square([width * 6, width * 2], center = true);
    else circle(width * 2);
} // end model
```

Making Model Circuits

Now that we have all the pieces, we can make some model circuits. Just to start, you may find it useful to use the full set of each type of gate (like the ones in Figure 7-2) as sort of plastic flash cards to remind yourself of the truth table of that gate. Then you can begin exploring combinations of the gates.

Gates as Combinations of Others

Gates, as mentioned earlier, can be constructed as combinations of other gates. This is a good way to get more fluency and intuition about the logical relationships among the gates. Some of these are called *De Morgan equivalents* after the 19th century British mathematician who first wrote them down.

As noted earlier, Peirce showed that NOR gates alone or NAND gates alone can be used to create any of the others (https://en.wikipedia.org/wiki/Logic_gate).

We create two equivalents here: AND, made up of NANDs (Figure 7-6 and Table 7-2), and OR, made up of NANDs (Figure 7-7 and Table 7-2). We can check that these work for all possible combinations with our models, or with a truth table. We show a combination here of one case with the models and the full truth table.

Figure 7-6. *AND gate made up of NANDs (inputs on bottom, output on top)*

Table 7-2. *Truth Table for Figure 7-6 (AND Made Up of NANDs)*

Input 1	Input 2	Output	Equivalent AND Output
0	0	0	0
1	0	0	0
0	1	0	0
1	1	1	1

Figure 7-7. *OR gate made up of NANDs (inputs on bottom, output on top)*

Table 7-3. *Truth Table for Figure 7-7 (OR Made Up of NANDs)*

Input 1	Input 2	Output	Equivalent OR Output
0	0	0	0
1	0	1	1
0	1	1	1
1	1	1	1

Flip-flop

One of the most basic logical components of a computer is the *flip-flop*, sometimes called an *S-R latch* (for *set-reset*) or *a bistable multivibrator*. Whatever we choose to call it, it is a way to store a single 1 or 0 (single bit) of information. You can read more about it at https://en.wikipedia.org/wiki/Flip-flop_(electronics).

The flip-flop shown in Figure 7-8 takes two inputs and, by feeding the outputs back into the opposite gate input, keeps its two outputs in opposite states from each other. Figure 7-8 is called an *SR NOR **latch***, because it is made up of two NOR gates with crossed feedback.

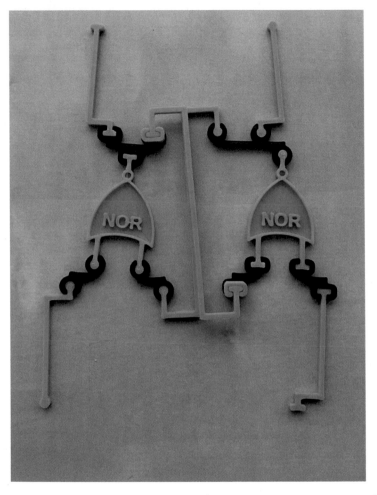

Figure 7-8. *Flip-flop with NOR gates (inputs on bottom, outputs on top)*

Figure 7-9 is a closeup of the crossed feedback paths, using a riser on each end of one of the feedback paths to keep the crossed paths separated with one passing over the other. Try building this circuit with several combinations of inputs. Note that having a pair of inputs that are both 1 is impossible to build in a static consistent way. In the flip-flop's stable states, the two inputs cannot both be 1. The outputs are always the opposite of each other.

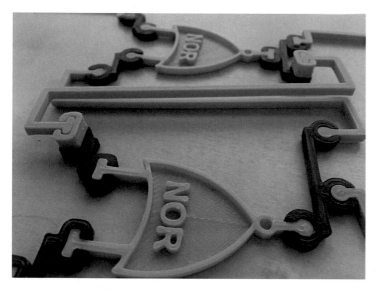

Figure 7-9. *Flip-flop showing crossover of feedback*

There are other variations of the flip-flop. Figure 7-10 uses NAND gates to accomplish the same thing, called an ***SR-bar NAND latch***. In this latch, the state with both inputs equal to 0 is not allowed.

Figure 7-10. *Flip-flop with NAND gates (SR-bar NAND)*

Try building these gates with the various possible outputs and see what happens to the two outputs (and when you start to "race" unstably back and forth on the feedback paths).

Adder

Another fundamental circuit in a computer is an adder. An ***adder*** is used to add two binary numbers—either two zeros, two ones, or one of each. When we add in binary, anything over 1 has to "carry" to the next digit, so adding requires keeping track of inbound carried values and outbound ones. Adders are typically cascaded (used in long sets with one feeding the next) to allow addition of many-bit numbers. Read more at `https://en.wikipedia.org/wiki/Adder_(electronics)`.

We have built a one-bit adder out of AND, OR, and XOR gates in Figure 7-11 and we have drawn the connections (with red lines being 0 and blue lines, 1) in Figure 7-12. It might be easier to see the connections in Figure 7-12 because some of the inputs have to cross others in Figure 7-11. Here is what is going on in both figures:

- We are adding the two values shown by the orangey-red and blue dots (at the bottom of the figure). Both of those are a 1, so the output should be 10 in binary (otherwise known as 2 in our base-10 system).

- The output value is noted by the yellow dot at the upper left. It is a zero, which is correct—when you add 1 + 1 in binary, you get a 0 plus a 1 to carry to the next place.

- The carry values are shown by green dots. The lower one is the value carried in (0 in this case), and the one at the top right is the value carried out to the next stage (1 in this case, because we are adding 1 and 1, which gives us a 1 to carry).

- For the physical system in Figure 7-11, we put white dots under the two places where the lines cross, because it is difficult to see in a 2D picture.

- We used a feedback connector to link the upper AND to the XOR in the upper right because the geometry worked out better that way, even though strictly speaking this is not a feedback loop.

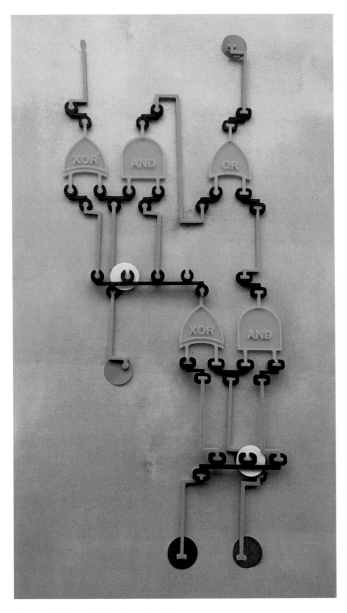

Figure 7-11. *Adder circuit with connectors*

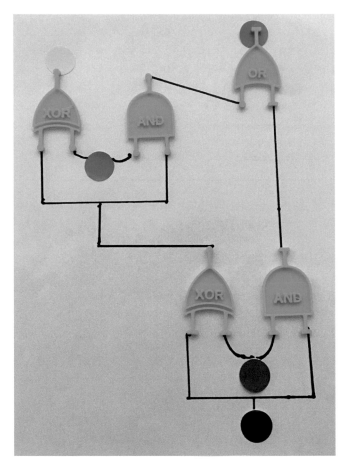

Figure 7-12. *Adder circuit, hand drawn*

In short, we have succeeded in showing that, in binary, $1 + 1$ equals 0 plus carry a 1 to the next digit, or $1 + 1 = 10$. Try tracing through this case to see how the logic plays out for different inputs.

The hand-drawn circuit is probably the way to go for anything this complex or beyond. We find the plastic pieces add value in keeping track of what you want the values at various points to be, but just drawing the circuits reduces the time required to make something. We found it helped to create a dot of the correct color where an input was going to connect and then draw the lines to those dots.

■ **Caution** We have found that as we build these logical structures it is easy to get engrossed with the physical part of the modeling. You may want to "look ahead" a little on paper so you do not get surprised by logical impossibilities (for instance, an output equal to 1 trying to connect to an input expecting a 0).

Logic diagrams lend themselves to a somewhat different topology than the convention of all inputs lined up on one side and all outputs on the right. Rather, you might want to think about what gates are in parallel with each other.

THINKING ABOUT THESE MODELS: LEARNING LIKE A MAKER

When we started working on these models, we thought we would be able to come up with cute mechanical equivalents of each gate, which might operate switches or rubber bands or some other simple part to "flow" a signal through a simulated circuit. We noted with amazement the complex mechanical logic gates we found online, which were difficult to understand and to validate. Then we discovered that the issue was that in some cases one had to store energy or a previous state in the circuit, in addition to the gates. For example, if a NOT gate gets a 0 as input, it has a 1 coming out. Thus, flow of whatever the analog of electricity is has to come from some reservoir somewhere. Mechanical gates might have been hard to print, too, and we try to make all our models as easy to print as possible.

We decided we would sacrifice complex inner workings for more somewhat duplicative parts and use a different part for different pairs of inputs for each gate. The next issue was the connectors—there needed to be connectors that could be used to lay out circuits with a variety of geometries, including the issue that each gate has an output in the middle that feeds into an input in the next gate that is offset from the center. In the end, we came up with the current connector set as a compromise that was not too complex but that would allow for some limited but interesting explorations, besides being flash cards of a sort.

Where to Learn More

A next step might be to try to create circuits with actual electronic components. Sparkfun has developed LogicBlocks Kits with individual gate components, described at https://learn.sparkfun.com/tutorials/logicblocks--digital-logic-introduction. These actually show the ones and zeros, with LEDs on each "gate" that are lit or not as appropriate.

You can also buy computer chips with several gates per chip, which expect to get an input signal on defined pins and will output the result on another defined pin. You may need to do some soldering for this option.

It is quite possible to simulate gates with fairly simple code, too. There are versions programmed in the Scratch visual programming environment, like this one: https://scratch.mit.edu/projects/66610/.

Teaching with These Models

Teaching circuit logic with actual components is always the ideal. However, these components might not be available if you are teaching Boolean logic in a software or math class, or if your budget is limited. You can use the models in this chapter as the basis of a very simple simulation of circuits with logic gates.

If you search the NGSS standards for a reference to *circuits*, the system responds with a note that the focus of the standards is on the idea of energy transfer, not types of circuits (www.nextgenscience.org/search-standards?keys=circuits), so we were not able to find any explicit guidance there. They note that circuits could be used in conjunction with teaching the Energy standards. These might be more appropriate to a math class or a coding class.

Project Ideas

The most obvious thing to do with this is to play with simulating circuits or, for that matter, the logic in various coding algorithms. You might try to lay out some classic simple computing algorithms. Most immediately, you can print out enough components to make two or three cascading steps for a multi-bit adder.

You might also consider how to use these pieces to teach simple logical constructs, and perhaps how to model and connect more-complex parts with multiple inputs and outputs. Perhaps there could be a group "Rube Goldberg Logic" exercise that starts with given inputs and branches out through gates (consistently!) to some planned end.

Summary

This chapter discusses what logic gates are and explores their role in binary computing. We create a set of simplified printable models of logic gates and "wires" of various sorts to connect them together. Then we use these components to create one gate in the form of combinations of other gates, along the way dealing with the problem of modeling wires that are crossing each other. Finally, we develop models of flip-flops and adders to create physical intuition of some of the foundational logical constructs of modern digital computing.

CHAPTER 8

■ ■ ■

Gravitational Waves

One of the biggest science stories of 2016 was the observation of **gravitational waves**. These waves were predicted by Einstein when he developed his theory of general relativity. We usually think about Isaac Newton when we think about gravity, with the (perhaps apocryphal) apple falling from a nearby tree as inspiration. In Newton's day and for a long time afterward, gravity was seen as a force that acted instantaneously no matter what the distance. If, say, the distance between two bodies changed, the entire universe would be affected by that change simultaneously.

However, when Einstein developed his theory of **general relativity**, things became a little more complicated. If the **gravitational field** around an object changes, those changes can only be felt by other bodies after the information travels at the speed of light. The information about those changes travels as **gravitational waves**, sometimes evocatively called "ripples in space-time."

LIGO

This all sounds like conventional astronomy so far—why not just look for gravity waves with a gravity telescope, just as you look for infrared light with an infrared telescope? Gravity does not really work that way. A better way to think about it would be using something very like an antenna to detect a gravity wave. *Radio astronomy*, which detects radio waves from objects in space, is the closest metaphor.

The "antenna" is called *LIGO*, for **Laser Interferometer Gravitational-Wave Observatory**. The LIGO project involves thousands of scientists all over the world, and two main instruments: very complex facilities in Hanford, Washington and Livingston, Louisiana (Figure 8-1).

© Joan Horvath and Rich Cameron 2017
J. Horvath and R. Cameron, *3D Printed Science Projects Volume 2*,
DOI 10.1007/978-1-4842-2695-7_8

Figure 8-1. *LIGO Livingston (courtesy Caltech/MIT/LIGO Laboratory)*

How Ligo Works

An *interferometer* compares two beams of light against each other, typically created by putting a laser beam through a *beam splitter*. One beam is turned 90 degrees by the beam splitter, and the other goes straight. Then the two beams are reflected back after they have traveled a distance (carefully designed to be almost identical) down arms at right angles to each other. The arms are at right angles because gravitational waves require what is called a *quadrupole antenna* for detection.

Depending on the phase shift between these two beams, the two beams interfere in a way that scientists can analyze and interpret. In the case of LIGO, the arms are 4 km long, and additional equipment is used to bounce the light back and forth about 280 times before it is combined with the other beam. (For a very detailed description with diagrams, see www.ligo.caltech.edu/page/ligos-ifo).

■ **Tip**   There is a 3D-printable model of interference between light passing through two slits in Chapter 2 of our ***3D Printed Science Projects*** (Apress, 2016), and Chapter 3 explores gravity, although on a solar-system scale, not an intergalactic one.

In the case of gravitational waves, though, the disturbances are so tiny that the instrument has to detect changes of about 10^{-19} meters, or 10,000 times smaller than the diameter of a proton. This involves elaborate means to both actively and passively damp out ambient vibrations (`www.ligo.caltech.edu/page/look-deeper`). The mirrors are hung on glass fibers to have minimum thermal disturbances, and the long arms of the interferometer are kept in vacuum. Elaborate mechanisms and optics tricks increase the apparent power of the laser and length of the arms of the interferometers.

LIGO is made up of two observatories across the United States from each other. The fact that they are 3002 km apart means that they will not detect the same ambient noises from traffic, seismic grumblings, and the like. The signal will appear at a very slightly different time at the two facilities, but it should vary with time the same way at the two places.

The Signal

Given all this, a gravitational wave has to come from a pretty major disturbance to be detectable at all. On September 14, 2015, both LIGO detectors observed the signal in Figure 8-2. ***Strain*** is a measure of how big the ripple that went by was, and the graphs show how this ripple varied over a fraction of a second.

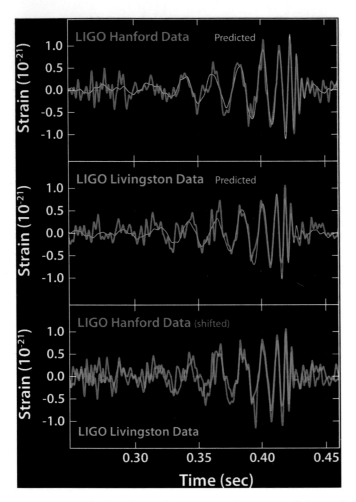

Figure 8-2. *The first detected gravitational wave signal, September 14, 2015 (courtesy Caltech/MIT/LIGO Laboratory)*

This is the entire event—LIGO has to take a lot of data to catch these tiny, ephemeral signals. The top two graphs show the signal at each station, and the bottom one the overlay allowing for the time difference of the signal's appearance. When a gravity wave goes by, space itself scrunches up and then expands. Even a giant event like this, though, only caused a space-time ripple less than a thousandth the radius of an atomic nucleus.

You can think of strain as the amount that space itself stretches (sort of like pulling a piece of fabric in one direction and seeing the fabric contract in the opposite direction.) Strain is a dimensionless, relative quantity—the amount something stretches divided by how big it was before you stretched it. Here the vertical axis is labeled in multiples of 10^{-21}—that means that if something was a meter long before the wave went by, the change in length would be only 10^{-21} m.

This signal (called GW150914) was caused by two black holes 1.3 billion light years away orbiting around each other faster and faster, and finally colliding. This is called an *inspiral*. LIGO caught the last fraction of a second during which these two black holes finally rotated faster and faster and fell into each other. The scientists call this type of signal a *chirp* (http://ligo.org/science/GW-Inspiral.php), and if made into an audio signal, it does indeed sound like a single tweet or boop. The power released by this is mind-boggling—about three times the mass of the sun was turned into energy in a fraction of a second. This is more power than the ***rest of the known universe*** put together emits. (See the "Where to Learn More" section in this chapter for references.)

We thought it would be exciting to create a 3D printed model of this inspiral system and the gravity waves it is creating. As you might imagine it was rather complicated. We were fortunate to meet some LIGO team members who were exhibiting their work at the American Association for Advancement of Science (AAAS) meeting in Boston in February 2016. They and, later, Alan Weinstein at Caltech were very helpful in pointing us to resources. We deeply appreciate that and the enormous amount of publicly available material the LIGO team has curated about their discoveries.

The Model

Many scientists are spending years creating models of gravitational waves. These are very complex models involving advanced math and physics. We looked at some "simple" papers. After wading through a few of them, we decided that we could only realistically develop a model that would *look like* an inspiral and exhibit some modest behaviorial similarities rather than trying to actually do a full model ourselves. What follows is our simple model, which will reflect broad-brush behavior of the system, if not the physics in detail.

Modeling the Amplitude and Frequency

Gravitational waves from a pair of black holes inspiraling will create a "chirp" signal, in which both the amplitude and frequency of the wave change over time. First we wanted to model this chirp. The signals in Figure 8-2 are how one would receive the signal at a fixed, distant point.

The graph in Figure 8-3 is what the signal would look like if you took an intergalactic instantaneous *snapshot* of the wave propagating at a particular time. (There is no way to do that, of course, because the speed of light is finite and different parts of the wave would get to an observer somewhere at different times, depending on the distance.) The model in Listing 8-1 generated Figure 8-1 in OpenSCAD (edited a bit in graphics programs afterward to add annotations).

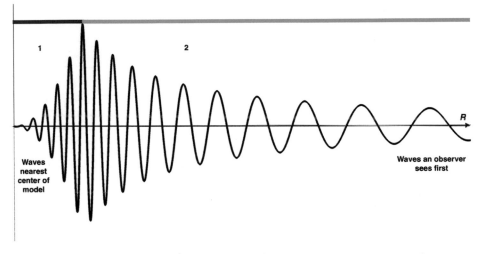

Figure 8-3. Our model of the chirp propagating (time is reversed from Figure 8-2)

Listing 8-1. Model to Explore Waveforms

```
// Graphing version of gravitational wave model.
// Rich Cameron, March 2017
// File gravityGraph.scad

a = 1/100; // Amplitude modifier
f = 2000; // Frequency modifier
offset = 0; // Time offset
trd = 150; // Ringdown time- time from peak amplitude to zero
res = .2; // Data point spacing

for(i = [0:res:1000]) hull() for(i = [i, i+res]) {
   translate([i, a * (
     (i < offset) ?
        0
     : (i < (offset + trd)) ?
        pow(i - offset, 2)
     :
        pow(trd, 2) * trd / (i - offset)
   ) * cos(f * (
     (i < (offset + trd)) ?
        (i - offset) / trd - 1
     :
        ln((i - offset) / trd)
   )), 0]) circle(1, $fn = 4);
}
```

150

```
for(i=[0:res:1000]) hull() for(i=[i, i+res]) {
    translate([i, 100 * ((
      (i<(offset+trd)) ?
        (i - offset) / trd - 1
      :
        ln((i - offset) / trd)
    )+1), 0]) circle(1, $fn=4);
} // End graphing model.
```

■ **Tip** The OpenSCAD model in Listing 8-1 generated the curve in Figure 8-3 by using OpenSCAD as a glorified graphing calculator. If you use OpenSCAD to create complex models, this is a good way to debug your math in the form OpenSCAD wants it before incorporating it in a model. Rich created the model in Listing 8-1 first to tweak the math before moving to the full model we see later on in the chapter.

Figure 8-3 shows the signal according to our model as the two black holes finish merging. The time from zero to the peak amplitude (the length of the red line in Figure 8-3, and the parameter trd in our models) is the ***ringdown time*** and is the time it takes for the black holes to merge completely and the disturbance to more or less disappear. Region 1 (the red bar) is the time after the black holes have merged; Region 2 (the green bar) is the runup to the collision as the black holes orbit around each other faster and faster (leading to the increasing amplitude and frequency of the gravitational waves generated). Thus, time as seen by a distant observer runs backwards in Figure 8-3—compare Figure 8-2, which shows the signal received on Earth.

Adding the Spiral

Next, we used this frequency and amplitude model and added a dependence on angle around the center, creating a curve that starts out as an Archimedean spiral and transitions to a logarithmic one (https://en.wikipedia.org/wiki/Logarithmic_spiral). This creates the spatial model of a snapshot in time of the waves emanating from the inspiral. Figure 8-4 shows the conventions used in this part of the model, in particular the radius r(x,y) and ***azimuth angle*** theta(x,y), both measured around the original center of mass of the two orbiting black holes. The radius will have units of time (represented in the physical model by a distance).

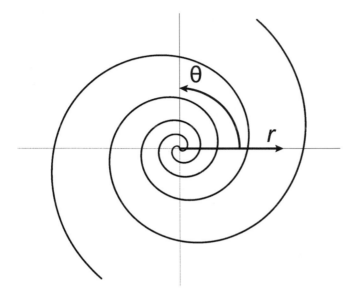

Figure 8-4. *The spiral component of the model*

■ **Caution**   The model in this chapter is a very simplified attempt to qualitatively replicate results that have been published based on sophisticated models. We did not attempt to actually obtain raw data and do any sophisticated curve fitting, but rather created functions by looking at the published chirp waveforms and measuring some key parameters manually from that. The math behind the actual models far exceeds what we could do in OpenSCAD as a practical matter. That said, the model is adequate to develop some simple intuition. See the "Where to Learn More" section for starting points in the popular and scientific literature based on LIGO results, and the "Projects" section for a discussion of the next steps one would take to improve upon this model.

There are several different aspects of the model that contribute to the height of the model's surface, *z*, at any point:

$$z = scaling\ factor * envelope\ function * wave\ of\ varying\ frequency\ and\ phase$$

Envelope function is a fancy way of saying that we selected simple curves that would give us the shape of the curves that outline the top (or bottom) of the wave in Figure 8-3. For the curve in Region 1 (under the red bar) in Figure 8-3, we use a parabola for the envelope function, and a constant frequency. For Region 2 (under the green bar), the envelope function is a hyperbola and the frequency varies logarithmically.

152

CHIRP MASS

Astrophysicists talk about a fundamental parameter of a binary black hole system called the *chirp mass*, defined relatively simply in Wikipedia at `https://en.wikipedia.org/wiki/Chirp_mass`. It relates the mass of the two bodies to the frequency of their rotation about each other and the rate of change of that frequency over time.

We did not tie the model in this chapter explicitly to chirp mass, other than to take some inspiration from the definition about the form of our approximations.

However, that might be a good next iteration, as we describe in the "Projects" section at the end of this chapter.

To make things easier to read in equation form, we will define T here (T is not used in the model). T is dimensionless, the difference between the time a signal will have propagated to a given radius minus the time represented by the `offset` (the time since the two black holes merged) divided by the time `trd`, the ringdown time:

$$T = (r(x,y) - \textit{offset}) / trd$$

We will also define a dimensionless constant C, which combines the model parameters a (scaling factor) and the square of `trd`:

$$C = a * trd^2$$

Now we will use all this to try to model the gravitational waves.

■ **Note**   To generate the behavior of the gravity waves generated by an inspiral, we wanted to show the double spiral of the two black holes drawing closer to each other. To do that we added a phase term of $2 * \theta$ (the factor of 2 gives two spiral arms in 360 degrees) to the model of the waveform in Figure 8-3. In our equations in this chapter, we use the symbol θ for `theta(x,y)`.

Model of Ringdown

In Region 1 (marked by the red bar) of Figure 8-3, the black holes have collided and are "ringing" at what we model as a constant frequency:

$$z = C * T^2 * cos(f * (T - 1) + 2 * \theta)$$

The parameter f is a constant frequency multiplier that for purposes of the model we can manipulate to compress or expand the spiral in the 3D print. (If you make f larger, more turns of the spiral will fit on your model. However, you may run into trouble because a high frequency will introduce sampling errors and may also produce features that are too small to print. You may also find that you want to lower your frequency and/or amplitude to reduce overhangs in the print.

> ■ **Note** The value of z is set equal to 0 to the left of the curve modeled in Region 1. In other words, we assume the gravity wave dies out to an undetectable level one ringdown time after the black holes merge and form their new supermassive single black hole.

Model of Inspiral

The waves generated while the black holes are approaching each other faster and faster is modeled in Region 2 (under the green bar) in Figure 8-3. If you were an observer on Earth, you would see the right side end of the wave in Figure 8-3 coming at first. We used an envelope function of $1/T$ in this region, and a logarithmic dropoff of frequency with radius. That gave us this equation:

$$z = C * (1/T) * cos (f * ln(T) + 2 * \theta)$$

Matching the Two Regions

Even though this is something of a "toy model" in that it does not use the complicated models from the real LIGO data, we wanted to be sure our two functions behaved well for reasonable values of the parameters. At the peak of the chirp, $T = 1$ (since at that point r(x,y) - offset = trd. If we put $T = 1$ into both these models, we get the same answer. We also checked that the frequency is the same across the break between regions. For those who know a little calculus, the derivative of the frequency is also constant, but the derivative of z with respect to T is not—because the functions change drastically at that point.

> ■ **Note** Listing 8-2 is the model incorporating these equations. This model uses some fairly complex OpenSCAD constructs to allow for the variety of different modeling regimes. See Appendix A for a discussion of OpenSCAD and links to its documentation.

Listing 8-2. The Inspiral Model

```
// Model of a gravitational wave caused by inspiraling black holes
// Rich Cameron, March 2017
// File gravityWave.scad
// Parts based on math function generator from
// 3D Printed Science Projects (Apress, 2016)

a=1/200; // amplitude scaling factor (for printing practicalities)
f=800;   // frequency scaling factor
offset=0;// Time offset (t=0 is when the black holes merge)
         // offset and trd should be positive numbers
trd=30; //  ringdown time
```

```
// r(x,y) is the radius of the model in units of time

// The next section is function modeling
// the waveform in each regime. Change this
// if you want a different curve fit.

function f(x, y)=a * (
   (r(x, y)<offset) ?
      0
   : (r(x, y)<(offset+trd)) ?
      pow(r(x, y) - offset, 2)
   :
      pow(trd, 2) * trd / (r(x, y) - offset)
) * cos(theta(x, y) * 2+f * (
   (r(x, y)<(offset+trd)) ?
      (r(x, y) - offset) / trd - 1
   :
      ln((r(x, y) - offset) / trd)
));

// The rest of the code takes the points f(x,y) and plots them
// for x and y from 0 to xmax-1 and 0 to ymax -1. Each increment
// is 1 mm. The plot is double-sided by default.
// If you change the model, you should not have to change
// anything below. You will need to scale your model appropriately
// to keep the wave amplitude manageable for a printed-sideways
// 3D print.

thick=4; // set to 0 for flat bottom
xmax=199;
ymax=199;
blocky=false; // if true, xmax and ymax must be less than 100.

toppoints=(xmax+1) * (ymax+1);
center=[xmax/2, ymax / 2];

function r(x, y, center=[xmax/2, ymax/2]) =
   sqrt(pow(center[0] - x, 2)+pow(center[1] - y, 2));
function theta(x, y, center=[xmax/2, ymax/2]) =
   atan2((center[1] - y), (center[0] - x));

// Now generate the surface points.
points=concat(
   [for(y=[0:ymax], x=[0:xmax]) [x, y, f(x, y)]], // top face
   (thick ? //bottom face
      [for(y=[0:ymax], x=[0:xmax]) [x, y, f(x, y) - thick]] :
      [for(y=[0:ymax], x=[0:xmax]) [x, y, 0]]
   )
);
```

```
zbounds = [min([for(i=points) i[2]]), max([for(i=points) i[2]])];

function quad(a, b, c, d, r=false)=r ?
   [[a, b, c], [c, d, a]]
:
   [[c, b, a], [a, d, c]]; //create triangles from quad

faces = concat(
   [for(
      bottom=[0, toppoints],
      i=[for(x=[0:xmax - 1],
      y=[0:ymax - 1]
   ) //build top and bottom
      quad(
         x+(xmax+1) * (y+1)+bottom,
         x+(xmax+1) * y+bottom,
         x+1+(xmax+1) * y+bottom,
         x+1+(xmax+1) * (y+1)+bottom,
         bottom
      )], v=i) v],
   // build left and right
   [for(i=[for(x=[0, xmax], y=[0:ymax - 1])
      quad(
         x+(xmax+1) * y+toppoints,
         x+(xmax+1) * y,
         x+(xmax+1) * (y+1),
         x+(xmax+1) * (y+1)+toppoints,
         x
      )], v=i) v],
   // build front and back
   [for(i=[for(x=[0:xmax - 1], y=[0, ymax])
      quad(
         x+(xmax+1) * y+toppoints,
         x+1+(xmax+1) * y+toppoints,
         x+1+(xmax+1) * y,
         x+(xmax+1) * y,
         y
      )], v=i) v]
);

if(blocky) for(i=[0:toppoints - 1]) translate(points[toppoints+i])
   cube([1.001, 1.001, points[i][2] - points[toppoints+i][2]]);
else rotate([90, 0, 0]) difference() {
   polyhedron(points, faces, convexity=5);
   //cube(200, center=true);
}

// echo(zbounds);
// echo(points);
// end model
```

The Time Offset

We have a parameter offset in the model. This parameter gives you the option of looking at the waves just as the ringdown time is ending (offset = 0) or later than that. Figure 8-5 is the result of the model in Listing 8-2 with offset = 0. Figure 8-6 is a snapshot at a later time, offset = 30. Because trd in this model is also set to 30, that means we are looking at the model after additional time equal to the ringdown time has gone by. The flat spot in the center reflects this.

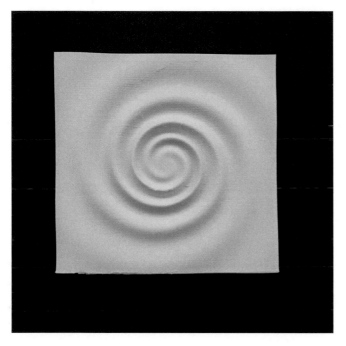

Figure 8-5. *The inspiral model just at the collapse (end of the chirp, as seen from Earth)*

■ **Note**   Figures 8-5 and 8-6 were both scaled down by a factor of 2 and rotated 45 degrees in the printer slicing software. The model defaults to 200 mm square prints.

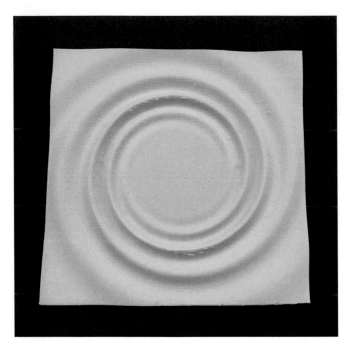

Figure 8-6. *Printed at two ringdown times after the black holes start to merge*

Printing and Changing the Model

These models are pretty straightforward to print. They print on their sides to get maximum resolution (Figure 8-7) and we recommend a brim so that the print does not fall over. Because they produce a 200 mm square print by default, you will probably need to scale them to fit on your printer. The models are double-sided—you can see both sides of the wave.

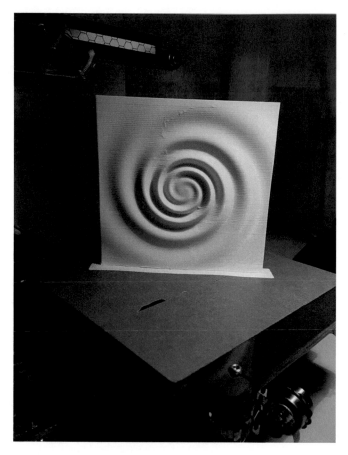

Figure 8-7. *The model printed vertically, with a brim*

We suggest you use the parameter values we have in Listing 8-2 to start, and not vary them too much. If you increase f you may start to have too small feature sizes. If you increase a you may get overhangs. You can play with the time offset and the ringdown time within small limits to see how those make the model vary.

■ **Note** The basic program is derived from our wave model in our first *3D Printed Science Projects* (Apress, 2016), Chapter 2, "Waves." The size of the model was increased to 200 mm square here, however, from 100 mm there. This was to allow better resolution for this wave.

If you would prefer to use different equations to fit the curves, you can change the section at the top of Listing 8-2. (If you are new to OpenSCAD and its conventions, see Appendix A.) The function in Listing 8-2 makes use of ***the ternary operator*** (a question mark and two values set off by a colon) to set values conditionally. You can think of this as an inline `if...else` statement, where the test is followed by a question mark, and the colon means "else." Here is an example:

`x = ((test) ? a : b)`

This means: if `test` evaluates to true, then x is set to a. If `test` evaluates to false, x is set to b. You can nest these, so that b could contain another conditional branch, and so on. The algorithm in Listing 8-2 is simpler than it looks; you just need to parse it carefully. This is the only way to do this type of conditional branching in OpenSCAD.

The frequency multiplier parameter f is not tied to the physical model, but again is a fit to make the model's geometry look right. You should think in terms of the plastic model you are making, and not necessarily an exact carryover of the numbers you would be manipulating in a computer model of the physics.

■ **Caution** OpenSCAD has some differences from the Java/C/Python code it resembles, notably a lack of traditional variables. See Appendix A and the OpenSCAD manual at `www.openscad.org`.

THINKING ABOUT THESE MODELS: LEARNING LIKE A MAKER

We saw the LIGO discovery and simulated images of the black hole and thought it would be a lot of fun to create this model. We thought that surely someone would have created some quick and dirty mathematical models that we could use to create this. However, when we chatted with some LIGO team members, we discovered that a theoretical physicist's idea of a "simple model" and ours were not the same thing. We found ourselves being referred to "quantum cosmology" papers, which are pretty much what you would expect.

The LIGO folks did, however, point us to the LIGO project's extensive resources and background materials. We did not find any closed-form wave equations, but we could stare at the signals and the existing inspiral simulations and figure out some simple curves that would give us some of the basic behavior. Rich even resorted to counting pixels in the images of the idealized waveforms to confirm that they were being modeled as a constant frequency in the ringdown phase.

We also drew on our experience with NACA airfoils in our first *3D Printed Science Projects* book. NACA airfoils are also modeled with a series of equations, and this model built on both that experience and our wave model, as we have noted elsewhere in the chapter.

And we learned a lot about black holes, gravity, and the challenges of measuring tiny signals. We hope you will do the same as you play with the model and some of the activities we point you to in the next section.

Where to Learn More

As befits a fundamental discovery, the LIGO project has curated many resources both for scientists and for the general public. There is a very good summary of the science at `www.ligo.org/science/Publication-GW150914/index.php`, which is based on the 2016 scientific paper by Abbott and many other authors, "Observation of Gravitational Waves from a Binary Black Hole Merger," which you can read for yourself at `https://doi.org/10.1103/PhysRevLett.116.061102`.

For a wide range of information, the LIGO project maintains several websites: `www.ligo.org`, `http://ligo.caltech.edu`, and `http://space.mit.edu/LIGO`.

Figure 8-8 might also help give you a sense of the scope of this discovery. For obvious reasons, black holes cannot be seen by conventional telescopes. Until now, their existence had been inferred from X-ray observations, or by light from other sources bending in a way that was suggestive of a black hole bending space and time. However, these black holes were smaller in size.

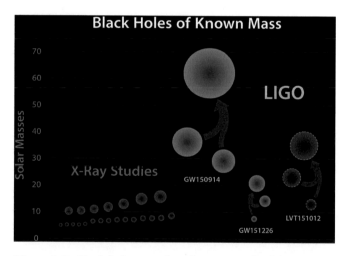

Figure 8-8. *Black hole mass chart (courtesy Caltech/MIT/LIGO Laboratory)*

The two LIGO-confirmed discoveries, and a third possible one, are shown on the right side of Figure 8-8. X-ray studies had found smaller pairs, but the massive ones that formed a new (even bigger) black hole were unprecedented in the data. There may be a lot of data and new discoveries to explore in the coming years.

Teaching with These Models

The LIGO project has developed an ***Educator's Guide***, which you can download from `www.ligo.caltech.edu/system/media_files/binaries/303/original/ligo-educators-guide.pdf`. They include a page of NGSS references for their materials, particularly ESS1.A—The Universe and Its Stars (`www.nextgenscience.org/dci-arrangement/1-ess1-earths-place-universe`).

The *Guide* has classroom activities to play with the concept of space-time, which they list as being appropriate for grades 5–12. One involves using checkerboard-patterned fabric to represent spacetime and putting some balls on it to show the distortions. We saw this at a conference, and it was surprisingly effective. If you want to try it on a grander scale, watch this video to see how it is done: `www.youtube.com/watch?v=MTY1KjeOyLg`.

If you teach near one of the LIGO sites (Hanford, Washington, and Livingston, Louisiana), as of this writing they have tours for school groups.

Project Ideas

The models themselves can be varied within a limited range of parameters. A sensible next step (if you have some calculus background) might be to wade into some of the research to see whether you can come up with a more sophisticated model. We note the concept of chirp mass in a sidebar earlier in the chapter.

Tying the model explicitly back to chirp mass in an accurate way and then being able to vary it to see what happens would be pretty amazing, but might be beyond what can be done practically with simple algebra equations (and thus, in OpenSCAD). Trying to make better and better models of these systems is of course the province of lots of graduate students worldwide, but we find you can always learn a lot through the attempt anyway.

It is possible to use OpenSCAD to plot a 3D surface from a set of data points; we do that in Chapter 1 of our first ***3D Printed Science Projects*** book. If you wanted to use data from a more sophisticated model, that would be an option too.

If you want to get involved in the actual science, you can participate in ***Einstein at Home*** (`https://einsteinathome.org`). This project uses spare time on your computer to process actual LIGO data. Or if you want to be more involved, you can classify data as a member of the Gravity Spy project at `www.zooniverse.org/projects/zooniverse/gravity-spy`.

Summary

Gravitational waves have recently been directly observed for the first time, as predicted by Einstein about a century earlier. The observations were made by the Laser Interferometer Gravitational-Wave Observatory (LIGO) Project. This chapter reviews the science and this discovery and develops a 3D-printable model of gravitational waves, specifically those from the first detection of the LIGO observatory. Gravitational waves are very mathematically complex. Here, we develop some simple curve-fits to the output of these complex models and create a model that can model some ranges of behavior of merging black holes. We also point to many resources and note projects that could be done starting with this model.

APPENDIX A

■ ■ ■

3D Printing and OpenSCAD

This book assumes that you know a little about 3D printing already. However, if you do not, this Appendix will get you started and give you resources to figure things out from here.

The 3D-Printing Process

First, we should say that you do not just "hit print." The amount of expertise and knowledge required is probably more analogous to cooking, or perhaps to using a sewing machine. 3D printing is rapidly evolving, too, so the details of what we say here may change, although we expect the basic ideas to stay the same for a while.

Having said all that, 3D printing requires three steps. Figure A-1 shows you the overall workflow for creating something with a 3D printer. This appendix concentrates on two free progams that together cover the three parts of creating a 3D print: making a 3D model (in this case, with OpenSCAD), "slicing" that model into layers, and then loading the sliced model onto a printer (with MatterControl for those latter two steps).

Figure A-1. *3D-printing workflow with OpenSCAD and MatterControl*

Filament-based 3D Printing

3D prints are created by melting plastic filament and then laying up that melted filament a layer at a time. Layers are very thin—typically 0.2 mm or so. Some types of printers use powder or liquid resins instead of filament. However, the models in this book are intended to be as easy as possible to print on 3D printers that use filament, like the one in Figure A-2 (a Deezmaker Bukito).

© Joan Horvath and Rich Cameron 2017
J. Horvath and R. Cameron, *3D Printed Science Projects Volume 2*,
DOI 10.1007/978-1-4842-2695-7

The spool of white material next to the printer is PLA (polylactic acid) filament, like that used for the prints in this book. PLA is a corn-based, biodegradable plastic that is one of the commonest materials for 3D-printing filament. Other common filament plastics, like ABS or PETG, should work fine as well, but we only tested the prints in PLA. Filament is typically sold on spools of 1 kg or 1 lb of material. The one in Figure A-2 is a 1 kg spool.

Figure A-2. *A filament spool and 3D printer*

File Types

The three steps required to create a 3D print correspond to three different types of file on your computer. In the case of the OpenSCAD 3D models in this book, the models are stored in files that end in .scad. When you are done working on the model in OpenSCAD, you save the final version in a .scad file and also *export* the file to one in the .stl format. The .stl format is a defacto standard for consumer 3D-printable models. Some vintages of Windows do not like the .stl suffix and think it is some sort of security file, but just ignore that and load the file into your slicing program.

For the next steps, MatterControl (or your printer's equivalent software) takes in an .stl file and outputs a .gcode file. The .gcode format (or an equivalent format, such as a .x3g file) is what actually runs on your printer. If your printer uses proprietary software, that software may or may not reveal this file to the user.

Next we will walk through OpenSCAD and MatterControl in turn, and give you pointers on getting started with each one.

■ **Tip** If you want more detail about 3D printing (including some discussion of post-processing your print or using 3D prints in the sand-casting process), you might consider Joan's book *Mastering 3D Printing* (Apress, 2014). If you want to focus on using the MatterControl software in particular and want more of a detailed user guide, you can instead get Joan and Rich's *3D Printing with MatterControl* (Apress, 2015). Both books review how to get started in 3D printing. See the MatterControl section of this Appendix to see how to tell whether MatterControl supports your 3D printer. If not, your 3D printer probably came with an equivalent proprietary program.

OpenSCAD

The OpenSCAD program allows you to develop models in a style that sort of looks like the C/Java/Python family of programming languages. It is free and open source, and we want to acknowledge and thank Marius Kintel and the many other contributors and maintainers of the program. You can look at any of the models in this book to see the syntax.

Downloading OpenSCAD

You can download OpenSCAD from www.openscad.org, and an excellent user manual is available at www.openscad.org/documentation.html. Download OpenSCAD and install it per the instructions on the download site. OpenSCAD is available in versions for Linux/UNIX, Windows, and macOS. The models in this book were tested with version 2015.03-3 for macOS. If you are a longtime OpenSCAD user and have an older version than that, you may need to update to the current version to be able to run the models in this book, which take advantage of some recently added features.

Editing the Models

Briefly, to edit one of the models in this book, you would proceed as follows. First, you would obtain the relevant .scad file for the model you are interested in. (See the Repositories note at the end of this appendix.)

Once you have the file and OpenSCAD is open, go to File ➤ Open and open the .scad file. If you do not see the model listing, go to View and uncheck Hide Editor so that you can see it. Now make any changes you feel you need to make and go to Design ➤ Preview to see if you have created what you had intended. Repeat until you think you are done.

■ **Tip** In OpenSCAD, Design ➤ Preview creates an object that you can view but cannot export. It is a lot faster than a full render, which can take a long time for some of the models in this book. Use this to preview models as you are making changes.

When you have your final model, go to Design ➤ Render to create a model that can be exported for 3D printing. Once you have compiled a file, you can export an .stl file. Go to File ➤ Export ➤ Export as STL. Figure A-3 is a screen shot of OpenSCAD with the flower from Chapter 6.

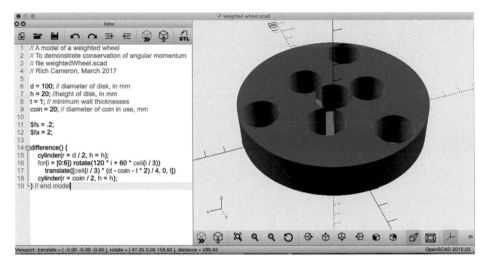

Figure A-3. *Screenshot of OpenSCAD*

Idiosyncrasies of OpenSCAD

If you are a programmer, OpenSCAD can be a little disconcerting because its syntax looks like that of the C/Java/Python family of languages. However, it is not a full programming language and has a few idiosyncracies.

The biggest one is that OpenSCAD does not have true variables, as one would define them in other programming languages. The variables in our models are best thought of as constants. You can assign another value to a variable, but (as would be true in algebra) y = y + 1 is ***not*** a valid statement in OpenSCAD. See the manual section on variables for details and examples at https://en.wikibooks.org/wiki/OpenSCAD_User_Manual/ General#Variables.

Functions in OpenSCAD are also functions in the mathematical sense. They return a value, but cannot perform other tasks beyond a single mathematical formula along the way. OpenSCAD has ***modules*** that are closer to what an experienced programmer will expect from a function.

In Chapter 8 we introduced the ternary operator (a question mark and two values set off by a colon) to set values conditionally. You can think of this as an inline if...else statement, where the test is followed by a question mark and the colon means "else." Here is an example:

```
x = ((test)? a : b)
```

This means: if test evaluates to true, then x is set to a. If test evaluates to false, x is set to b. You can nest these, so that b could contain another conditional branch, and so on. OpenSCAD does not support if...then...else statements for branching based on a variable.

MatterControl

Once you have exported your .stl file from OpenSCAD, you need to run a program that can convert the model into commands to drive your 3D printer. We will describe the MatterControl program here, which is a free and open source program supported by our friends at MatterHackers. MatterControl is compatible with many types of 3D printer. There are, however, some proprietary ones that do not use the same standard as others.

Printers MatterControl Supports

The list of printer models that are officially supported by MatterControl can be found at www.mattercontrol.com/#jumpSupportedModels. (If your printer is not listed there, MatterControl does not include settings for it, but you should be able to configure it to work with any printer that uses .gcode files). If your printer is not supported by MatterControl, your manufacturer likely has created a proprietary program that will also take an .stl file as its input. Check your manufacturer's documentation, or contact MatterHackers to see if an existing 3D printer profile can be used for your machine.

Downloading and Installing MatterControl

Assuming that your printer is supported, you can download MatterControl at www.mattercontrol.com, in versions for Mac OS X, Windows, and Linux. There is some documentation linked to the download page (as of this writing, through a link entitled Learn More).

Using MatterControl

MatterControl is a very capable and complex program. To take full advantage, you can use their online documentation, or get a copy of our book on MatterControl that we noted earlier. This section will give you a very quick guide to getting started.

First, you will need to tell MatterControl what type of 3D printer you have. On the home screen, you can use the File ➤ Add A Printer item and its subsequent dialogs to set up your printer. Some printers need to be actively connected to a computer, and some can run off an SD card or wireless connection. See MatterHackers' documentation and your manufacturer's suggestions for this step.

Once you have your printer squared away, you will need to load in an .stl file. You can either use the +Add button on the lower left of Figure A-4 or the menu item File ➤ Add File to Queue (that is, import an .stl file to be printed), as shown in Figure A-4.

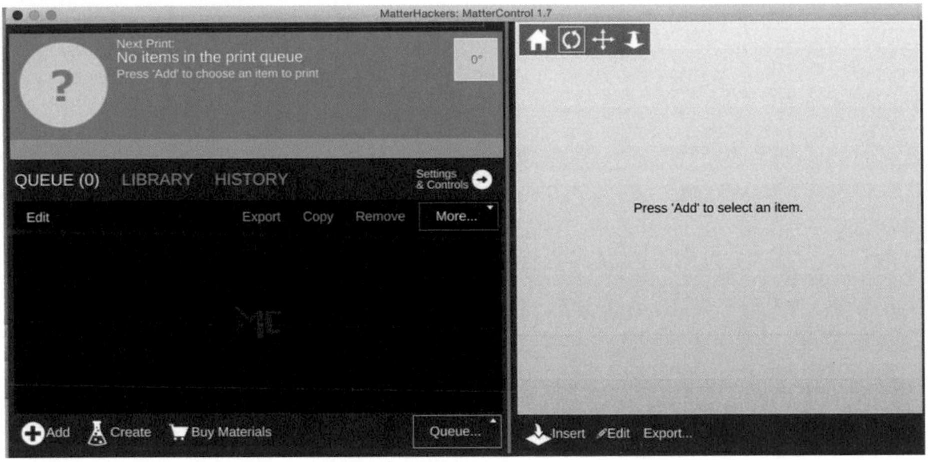

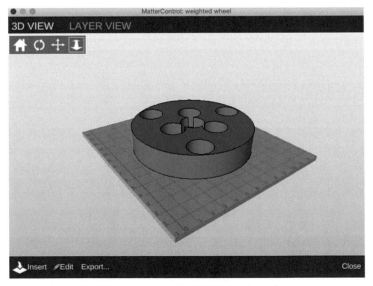

Figure A-4. *The MatterControl home screen*

If you mouse over an item in the queue (the weighted wheel from Chapter 5, in this case), you will see two options: View and Remove. Remove removes the file from the queue (deletes it from MatterControl's queue, in other words). View starts the process of preparing the file to print.

After you click View, you will see a screen like that in Figure A-5. The screen that comes up (3D VIEW) shows your print as it will lie on your 3D printer's print bed. If it is hanging off the ends or otherwise problematic, there are tools you can use (after clicking Edit) to rectify the problems. When you are done, be sure to click Save to save your changes before the final creation of your printable file.

Figure A-5. *The View screen, with 3D VIEW selected*

Once you are done editing and are satisfied that the file is ready to 3D print, select LAYER VIEW. The program will ask you to click Generate if you have not generated your printable file yet. This step breaks the model into layers that can be printed and creates the commands that will move around the print head and push filament where it needs to be. You can see the LAYER VIEW screen in Figure A-6. The LAYER VIEW screen also tells you how long the print will take, more or less, and how much filament (3D-printing raw material) it will use up.

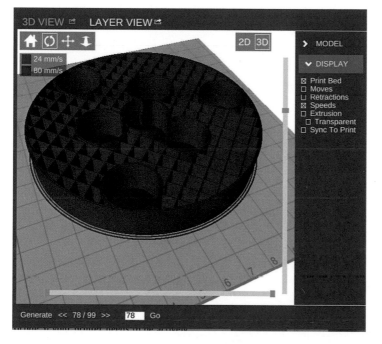

Figure A-6. *The View screen, with LAYER VIEW selected*

If this looks good, go back to the home screen (Figure A-4) and click Export (in the middle of the screen). Then select Export as Gcode. If your printer needs to be actively connected to a computer, at this point you could send the file to the printer.

Settings

Hypothetically, the discussion thus far should just work as stated, and you will have gone from a model in this book to a physical one in your hand. Real life with a 3D printer is not always that simple, though. 3D printers have a lot of different settings, because tweaking is needed sometimes. If you click the Settings & Controls button on the home screen (Figure A-4), you will find yourself at a page like the one in Figure A-7.

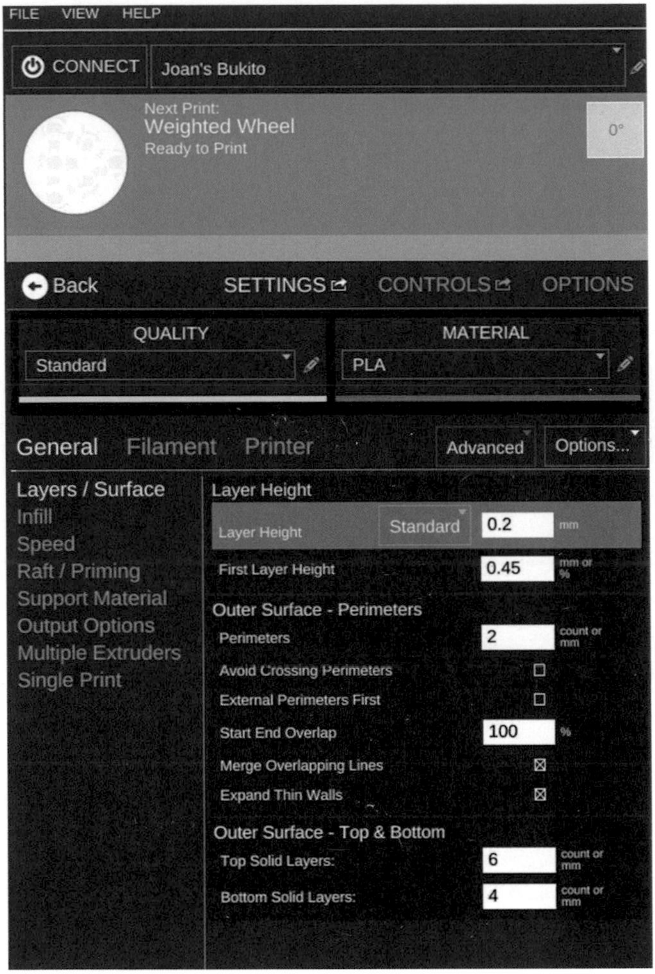

Figure A-7. *The Settings & Controls screen*

In Figure A-7 you see SETTINGS, CONTROLS, and OPTIONS. Probably as a beginner you will not touch anything in OPTIONS except for perhaps selecting MatterSlice as your Slice Engine, if it has not already defaulted there. CONTROLS are functions you will use to interact with your printer to solve a problem or set up your printer, which we will not explore here.

That leaves SETTINGS. The models in this book were, for the most part, designed to be as simple to print as possible. That means that you should be able to get away with pretty generic settings. We will talk now about some that you might need to change, particularly General ➤ Support Material and General ➤ Skirt and Raft.

Support

Because a filament-based 3D printer builds up prints from a platform, if a piece sticks out sideways higher up on a print, that part will just fall down if *support material* is not built ahead of time to support it. The models in this book should not need support to print. You can look in the LAYER VIEW to see if it looks like the overhangs will be too large to manage without support.

The rule of thumb is that a slope can overhang by about 45 degrees before support is necessary. However, sometimes you can push your luck. If you do need to add support, check the Generate Support Material box under General ➤ Support Material. In general, the less support you have to generate (and then pick off), the better. If you have something really complex, you may have to check the Support Everywhere box. That creates support as needed, including in nooks and crannies of the model where it may be hard to remove. Be sure to preview your model in LAYER VIEW first to see how it looks.

■ **Note**   MatterControl will not show support in the 3D VIEW. It does not generate the support until layers are generated for the LAYER VIEW.

Raft

The models in this book were designed not to depend on your printer's bed being smooth and flat. However, should you encounter that situation in the future, if your printer's bed is not very flat you can print these parts on a raft. A *raft* is a thin layer that prints first on the platform, and then the model prints on top of it. If things are not fitting together well, adding a raft (General ➤ Skirt and Raft) is an option. You will need to remove the raft, though, which may be difficult to do cleanly if your raft settings have not been tuned to allow it to release from the print. You may want to test it with a smaller piece to make sure the raft will peel away in one piece before printing a larger model on a raft.

You will notice in the same grouping of settings some choices referring to a skirt. A *skirt* is a line drawn around the model's first layer to prime the nozzle. If you make a skirt attached (or 0 mm away from the model) it is usually called a *brim* (as in hat brim). A brim can help hold prints onto the print bed, though it will not help flatten the bottom of a print the way a raft will.

■ **Caution**   If you change a setting, be sure to click SAVE in the SETTINGS window before going back to the LAYER VIEW window and generating a new printable file. Otherwise, it is easy to accidentally revert any unsaved settings.

Other Considerations and Alternatives for These Models

For the most part, these models were printed in PLA with a layer height of 0.2 mm (General ➤ Layers/Surface) or in some cases 0.1 mm. Your printer defaults may be different than this, and you may want to do a few tests with one of our simpler prints to establish your favorite basic settings.

We also have used the Cura open source slicing program (`https://ultimaker.com/en/products/cura-software`) for some of the models in this book. Even though it is on a 3D-printer manufacturer's site, it too works for many printers.

Archives and Repositories

There is a link for the source for the OpenSCAD models on this book's copyright page, and also linked to the book's page at our publisher, `www.apress.com/us/book/9781484226940`. The files archived there are the ones shown in the book. In addition, we have a repository that may have more current versions at `https://github.com/whosawhatsis/3DP-Science-Projects-V2`.

If you develop any new models around these, we hope you will add them to the open source repositories and help build out a community of scientific learners.

APPENDIX B

■ ■ ■

Links

About the Authors

Nonscriptum LLC: www.nonscriptum.com

Chapter 1. Pendulums

Apress: www.apress.com

Coupled Pendulum video: www.youtube.com/watch?v=izy4a5erom8

Double Pendulum video: www.youtube.com/watch?v=AwT0k09w-jw

Forces and Interactions science standards: www.nextgenscience.org/topic-arrangement/msforces-and-interactions

Thingiverse: www.thingiverse.com

Moment of Inertia on Wikipedia: https://en.wikipedia.org/wiki/Moment_of_inertia#Compound_pendulum

Simple Harmonic Motion on Wikipedia: https://en.wikipedia.org/wiki/Simple_harmonic_motion

Pendulums on Wikipedia: https://en.wikipedia.org/wiki/Pendulum

Kater's Pendulum on Wikipedia: https://en.wikipedia.org/wiki/Kater's_pendulum

NASA GRACE mission: http://grace.jpl.nasa.gov/mission/gravity-101/

Foucault Pendulum on Wikipedia: https://en.wikipedia.org/wiki/Foucault_pendulum

Chapter 2. Geology

Anticline photo: www.sciencebase.gov/catalog/item/51dd7db8e4b0f72b4471b201

Syncline photo: www.sciencebase.gov/catalog/item/51dc3902e4b0f81004b7a61a

Barchan dune photo: www.sciencebase.gov/catalog/item/51dd88f3e4b0f72b4471c140

© Joan Horvath and Rich Cameron 2017
J. Horvath and R. Cameron, *3D Printed Science Projects Volume 2*,
DOI 10.1007/978-1-4842-2695-7

Barchan dune crest photo: www.sciencebase.gov/catalog/item/51dd894ee4b0f72b447 1c19a

Summary of aeolian processes on Mars and Titan: www.planetary.org/blogs/guest-blogs/2015/0326-lpsc-2015-aeolian-processes-mars-titan.html

Photo of barchan dunes on Mars: www.uahirise.org/ESP_014404_1765

Types of dunes: www.nps.gov/grsa/learn/nature/dune-types.htm

Geological Society: www.geolsoc.org.uk

Earth's Systems science standards: www.nextgenscience.org/pe/ms-ess2-2-earths-systems

Geologist William Smith on Wikipedia: https://en.wikipedia.org/wiki/William_Smith_(geologist)

Strike and dip on Wikipedia: https://en.wikipedia.org/wiki/Strike_and_dip

Terrain2STL: http://jthatch.com/Terrain2STL/

Moon2STL: http://jthatch.com/Moon2STL/.

The U.S. Geological Survey's education site: http://education.usgs.gov

Syncline and anticline clay models: http://jazinator.blogspot.com/2010/05/teaching-folds-using-play-doh.html

Chapter 3. Snow and Ice

Gallery of snow crystals: www.snowcrystals.com

Snowflake machine: www.thingiverse.com/thing:1159436

Fixed-volume objects: www.youmagine.com/designs/fixed-volume-objects

"Snowflake Growth Successfully Modeled from Physical Laws": www.scientificamerican.com/article/how-do-snowflakes-form

Motion and Stability: Forces and Interactions science standards: www.nextgenscience.org/dci-arrangement/hs-ps2-motion-and-stability-forces-and-interactions

Earth's systems science standards: www.nextgenscience.org/pe/5-ess2-2-earths-systems

Salt on Wikipedia: https://en.wikipedia.org/wiki/Salt

Video of an iceberg rolling: https://youtu.be/mvQ4eDKf9UY

Cavalieri's Principle: https://en.wikipedia.org/wiki/Cavalieri's_principle

Snowflakes on Wikipedia: https://en.wikipedia.org/wiki/Snowflake

Larsen Ice Shelf on Wikipedia: https://en.wikipedia.org/wiki/Larsen_Ice_Shelf

Archimedes' Principle: https://en.wikipedia.org/wiki/Archimedes'_principle

Chapter 4. Doppler and Mach

Waves and Their Applications science standards: `www.nextgenscience.org/pe/hs-ps4-1-waves-and-their-applications-technologies-information-transfer`

Ernst Mach's contribution to science and philosophy: `https://plato.stanford.edu/entries/ernst-mach/`

Fourier Transforms on Wikipedia: `https://en.wikipedia.org/wiki/Fourier_transform`

Redshift on Wikipedia: `https://en.wikipedia.org/wiki/Redshift`

Chapter 5. Moment of Inertia

Fidget Spinner: `www.thingiverse.com/thing:1802260`

Forces and Interactions science standards: `www.nextgenscience.org/topic-arrangement/hsforces-and-interactions`

Mythbusters slow-motion sneeze video: `www.discovery.com/tv-shows/mythbusters/videos/slow-motion-sneezes/`

Moment of Inertia on Wikipedia: `https://en.wikipedia.org/wiki/Moment_of_inertia`

PhysicsLAB: `http://physicslab.org`

Chapter 6. Probability

The Khan Academy: `www.khanacademy.org`

Pinwheel Dice Set with Decader set by Chuck Stover: `www.shapeways.com/product/DKP3VVFL8/pinwheel-dice-set-with-decader?optionId=43314776`

Correlation: `www.mathsisfun.com/data/correlation.html`

Heredity and Variation of Traits science standards: `www.nextgenscience.org/dci-arrangement/hs-ls3-heredity-inheritance-and-variation-traits`

Statistics and Probability Common Core standards: `www.corestandards.org/Math/Content/HSS/introduction/`

Bivariate data Common Core standards: `www.corestandards.org/Math/Content/8/SP/A/1/`

Pearson Correlation Coefficient on Wikipedia: `https://en.wikipedia.org/wiki/Pearson_correlation_coefficient`

Multivariate Normal Distributions on Wikipedia: `https://en.wikipedia.org/wiki/Multivariate_normal_distribution`

Correlation Coefficient on Wolfram Mathworld: `http://mathworld.wolfram.com/CorrelationCoefficient.html`

Chapter 7. Digital Logic

Binary Arithmetic on Khan Academy: www.khanacademy.org/math/algebra-home/alg-intro-to-algebra/algebra-alternate-number-bases/v/number-systems-introduction

Binary Arithmetic on Ryan's Tutorials: http://ryanstutorials.net/binary-tutorial/binary-arithmetic.php

Science standards relating to circuits: www.nextgenscience.org/search-standards?keys=circuits

Logic Gates on Wikipedia: https://en.wikipedia.org/wiki/Logic_gate

Flip-Flops on Wikipedia: https://en.wikipedia.org/wiki/Flip-flop_(electronics)

Adders on Wikipedia: https://en.wikipedia.org/wiki/Adder_(electronics)

LogicBlocks kits: https://learn.sparkfun.com/tutorials/logicblocks--digital-logic-introduction

Scratch Logic Kit: https://scratch.mit.edu/projects/66610/

Chapter 8. Gravitational Waves

Laser Interferometer Gravitational-Wave Observatory: www.ligo.caltech.edu/page/ligos-ifo

LIGO vibration damping: www.ligo.caltech.edu/page/look-deeper

OpenSCAD: www.openscad.org

Summary of LIGO science: www.ligo.org/science/Publication-GW150914/index.php

"Observation of Gravitational Waves from a Binary Black Hole Merger": https://doi.org/10.1103/PhysRevLett.116.061102

Ligo Scientific Colaboration: www.ligo.org

Caltech LIGO project site: http://ligo.caltech.edu

MIT LIGO project site: http://space.mit.edu/LIGO

LIGO Educator's Guide: www.ligo.caltech.edu/system/media_files/binaries/303/original/ligo-educators-guide.pdf

Earth's Place in the Universe science standards: www.nextgenscience.org/dci-arrangement/1-ess1-earths-place-universe

Fabric and hoop gravity visualization video: www.youtube.com/watch?v=MTY1KjeOyLg

Gravity Spy project: www.zooniverse.org/projects/zooniverse/gravity-spy

Gravitational wave inspiral description: http://ligo.org/science/GW-Inspiral.php

Logarithmic Spirals on Wikipedia: https://en.wikipedia.org/wiki/Logarithmic_spiral

Chirp Mass on Wikipedia: https://en.wikipedia.org/wiki/Chirp_mass

Einstein@Home: https://einsteinathome.org

Appendix A. 3D Printing and OpenSCAD

OpenSCAD manual: www.openscad.org/documentation.html

List of printer models that MatterControl supports: www.mattercontrol.com/#jumpSupportedModels

Apress page for this book: www.apress.com/us/book/9781484226940

OpenSCAD variables: https://en.wikibooks.org/wiki/OpenSCAD_User_Manual/General#Variables

Cura software: https://ultimaker.com/en/products/cura-software

Models from this book on Github: https://github.com/whosawhatsis/3DP-Science-Projects-V2

Index

A

Adder circuit, 139
Angular velocity, 83, 84
Anticline model
    oil exploration, 25
    OpenSCAD model, 31
    printing, 26
Anticline model, 24
Archimedean spiral, 151
Archimedes' principle, 66
Archived sites, 172

B

Bagnold, R.A., 40
Barchan model, 41, 42, 48
Beam splitter, 146
Binomial coefficient, 105, 116
Bistable multivibrator, 135
Black holes, 149, 151, 160, 161
Boolean operations, 117
Brim, 36
Brute force method, 113

C

Centimeter-gram-second (cgs) units, 85
Chirp mass, 153
Cooling tower, 107
Coupled pendulums, 7

D

Damping force, 3
De Morgan equivalents, 133

D

Dip direction, 30
Doppler, Christian, 69
Doppler effect, 69
Doppler shift, 69
    frequency shift, 70
    model of, 71
    related of redshift, 81
Double pendulum, 14, 19
Dunes, 23, 38
    angle of repose, 39
    barchan model, 38, 41, 42
    blown sand, 40
    desert dunes, 40
    on Mars and Titan, 46
    OpenSCAD Model, 44

E

Einstein, Albert, 145
Envelope function, 152

F

Factorial function, 105
Feedback wires, 122
Fidget spinner, 93
Folding, 23
Foucault pendulum, 20
Fourier transforms, 76, 81
Frustrum model, 55

G

Galilei, Galileo, 2
General relativity theory, 145
Geology, 23

© Joan Horvath and Rich Cameron 2017
J. Horvath and R. Cameron, *3D Printed Science Projects Volume 2*,
DOI 10.1007/978-1-4842-2695-7